Sweet Dreams, Tanya

By
Danielle Tanner

Kingdom Publishers

Sweet Dreams Tanya
Copyright© Danielle Tanner

All rights reserved. No part of this book may be reproduced in any form by photocopying or any electronic or mechanical means, including information storage or retrieval systems, without permission in writing from both the copyright owner and the publisher of the book. The right of Danielle Tanner to be identified as the author of this work has been asserted by her in accordance with the Copyright, Designs and Patents Act 1988 and any subsequent amendments thereto.

A catalogue record for this book is available from the British Library.

All Scripture Quotations have been taken from the New King James, NIV and the New American Standard Bible

ISBN: 978-1-911697-54-1

1st Edition by New Leaf Publishing

2nd Edition by Kingdom Publishers, London, UK.

You can purchase copies of this book from any leading bookstore or email
contact@kingdompublishers.co.uk

DEDICATION

To my English teacher David, who many years ago suggested I write.
Between you and me, I thought you were delirious.

To my husband Anton, and brother Serge, for their unflinching support
and belief that "Yes, you can do it!"

To all those who planted seeds in me and helped me be a 'good ground'
able to bear fruit and produce a hundred (Mark 4:20). Today, I can say,
"I'm fruitful."

And thank You, Lord, for the grace to complete this.

Contents

DEDICATION	5
Chapter I | The Encounter	9
Chapter II | Dealing with 'Goliath' Greg	19
Chapter III | The Shocking Discovery	30
Chapter IV | The Boy Jesus in the Temple and Pastor Ben Rescued	38
Chapter V | Grove Park, Lewisham	47
Chapter VI | Raising the Alarm	58
Chapter VII | Confronting the Past	69
Chapter VIII | Ada's Hair Studio	79
Chapter IX | Saving Baby Moses	89
Chapter X | 'Cast the First Stone!'	100
Chapter XI | Young Solomon's Request for Wisdom	110
Chapter XII | Hotel Arrival	120
Chapter XIII | The Night before the First Audition	130
Chapter XIV | Meeting Divine	141
Chapter XV | First Auditions	152
Chapter XVI | The Mirror Game	163

Chapter XVII | The Second Round of Auditions   175

Chapter XVIII | Young David Chosen to be King   185

Chapter XIX | Second Chance   197

Chapter XX | Esther Becomes the Queen   209

Chapter XXI | The Final Audition   220

Chapter XXII | Home Sweet Home   230

Chapter XXIII | Confession Time   243

Chapter XXIV | Made in Chelsea   255

Chapter XXV | The Sea of Forgetfulness   266

Chapter XXVI | The Kairos Moment   278

Chapter I | The Encounter

"Wake up, Tanya, it's time to get ready for your online class."
"Mhmm," was the only response.

Keisha knew that she would have to shake her fourteen-year-old to wake her up, as she was a deep sleeper and had hearing issues. It would usually take four or five attempts before Tanya actually got up.

There was no commute to school or to work due to the pandemic. The school had opted to conduct its classes online, for the foreseeable future, for the safety of its pupils. It was a modern school, and they had the necessary facilities to do so. Staying at home had both benefits and inconveniences. It meant that Keisha didn't have to drop her child at St. Nicholas' School, then go to work by car or catch the train to Stratford. The downside was that Tanya would invariably spend time speaking to her friends on Zoom or WhatsApp, or surf online for hours. How on earth they managed to do that surreptitiously with her still in the house was a mystery. Keisha had to install, on the advice of the school, software to monitor and block access to any unwanted or inappropriate websites that Tanya might access.

"Come on, Tee! You need to get washed and dressed; breakfast is ready."

She sometimes called her baby girl Tee. But Tanya preferred people not to use the short version of her first name; the only exception was her mother.

"I've prepared your favourite smoothie," she said quickly over her shoulders to lure Tanya out of bed as she was going back downstairs. She was probably famished – a banana, blackberry, and spinach smoothie would go down a treat.

A moment later, Tanya was wide-awake and saying her prayers. After a quick shower, she joined her mum at the breakfast table in the kitchen.

"Mummy, I had another one of my dreams. This time I dreamt of Jonah in the whale."

"Jonah wasn't in a whale," she replied, "he was in a great big fish."

Keisha was not surprised by her daughter's dream, as this was a common occurrence. Her daughter regularly had dreams of Bible characters, often after she read a passage in the scripture.

"Remember, it's our games night with Audrey Blanchard's dad and Ana Ramos's mother is taking part as well," Tanya said.

"Shoot, I almost forgot!" She knew she could not get out of it. The girls loved it. She did too, but she was so busy at work.

Later on, Keisha heard Tanya sharing the dream with her school friends and smiled. None of Tanya's friends knew much about the Bible; this was a golden opportunity for her to speak about something that really mattered to her. She was an avid reader of the Lions Children's Collection, which had tons of Bible staples in it. She was a good storyteller; a talent she had acquired from a very young age. Keisha allowed her to indulge. It was her favourite pastime, aside from dreaming of Bible heroes. She remembered how, as a child, she used to love reading and would spend many sleepless nights hiding beneath the blanket, using a torch to decipher the words. She was an '80s-born native of Atlanta, Georgia, the home city of CNN. The summers were hot and humid. She did not miss the humidity.

Keisha had graduated *Summa Cum Laude* in Biology from Georgia State University and obtained a scholarship to study abroad. While she excelled at school, at home, things were a little different. Her mum was a struggling single mother working as a shop assistant. She tried to juggle two jobs. Her relationship with her mum was difficult back then.

"Why don't you get a job and help me with the bills," she would often say.

"Mum, my mentor says I should focus on my studies. He says if I study hard and get good grades, I will get a scholarship."

They constantly argued about it, so Keisha liked to stay at school to avoid trouble. She was studying so hard she did not have time to date or party. Things had improved a lot between them since then. Keisha had made a couple of brief visits throughout the years. However, these had lessened over the last ten years; Keisha's mum had not been able to travel due to poor health, so Tanya's memories of her grandmother had become vague. She seldom spoke of her.

As for her own dad, Frederick 'Fred' Campbell, her mum told her that he died in a car accident when she was a baby. She knew very little of her father's side of the family. They had never cared to ask of her. She was brought up single-handedly by her mother without them being concerned enough to find out how they were faring. She was aware that there was some Cherokee blood on her paternal side, but that was about it.

She had done everything in her power to give Tanya a different upbringing, always ensuring that her daughter never lacked love, care, or affection. But she was fully aware that a father figure was ostensibly missing from her daughter's life. This was the reason she liked Pastor Martin or Assistant Pastor Kweku to contribute as much as possible to her daughter's education. However, she was painfully aware that it could not fill the vacuum that her sweet and loving daughter sometimes complained about. And try as much as she could, she could never replace or fill that void.

These were now distant memories. But some memories were best left behind. They were living in London, England at present. It was surprising that Keisha had lost her Atlantan accent and sounded more British by the day.

It was time to get to work. She had the training to organise for the new starters and then a Microsoft Teams meeting to attend. This was going to be a busy day. She had the brilliant idea of preparing some spicy vegetable and lentil soup for lunch the night before, so she wouldn't be under pressure during the day. That was at least one thing she could tick off her to-do list.

From time to time, she would check on Tanya to make sure that she was attending her online classes. She excelled at school, but could sometimes be distracted. She slowly opened the door and saw the teen listening attentively to the instructions of her teacher. Keisha thought that she worried herself too much for nothing over Tanya.

Then, once the class was over, it was time for the online team game. There were three teams. The first team was team A: Audrey and her father, Julien. Team B was made up of Ana and Sofia. Keisha and Tanya were team C. Ana and her mother were from Salamanca, Spain, while Audrey and her dad were from Paris. It was the cultural differences that most likely brought them together. Ana had a strong Spanish accent, while Audrey's accent was not as strong – but still, one could tell that she wasn't a native of London.

"Hello, everyone," said Sofia.

"Hi," responded Julien.

"Hey, guys." Keisha was attempting to be cheerful, but did not sound too convincing.

"Ooh, you sound very tired," said Julien with a very strong French accent.

"Yeah, it's been very busy at work."

"Well, it's time to relax now. Let's forget about work. I have a very interesting game for us today," Sofia said, delighted with herself.

"What's the name of the game?" asked Audrey.

"It's called Kahoot."

"Oh, I know that game. We sometimes play it at work."

"Yes, but I have chosen Kahoot for students."

"What's Kahoot?" Tanya asked, a bit lost.

"It's a game with multiple choice quizzes and trivia. But I have tailored it to you youngsters so that it's not too hard. You'll see, you'll enjoy it! Let's start."

Audrey was the most enthusiastic. She was really good at quizzes, and she had a very competitive spirit. The *youngsters* would be the main players with a little help from their respective parents.

Ana had prepared about forty questions. "The team with the highest number of correct answers will win. The game will last about fifty minutes as Keisha and Tanya have to go to their choir practice."

At the end of the game, Ana and Sofia came out on top while Tanya and Keisha came last.

Audrey was very upset at not having won. "That's not fair, you asked questions that you and Ana already knew," she accused Sofia.

"That's not the case, Audrey."

"But it's true. You know that Ana is very good at maths, and your quiz had loads of calculations."

"That's good, Audrey," said her father. "It was meant for you to use your brains."

"Mais papa," she said in French. Audrey liked to pepper her conversations with French words.

"Taratata, calm down, Audrey," responded her dad. "That's enough now. You need to get over it." He then explained to the others that Audrey could be a bad loser at times. They all started laughing. And that is when Audrey realised that she had taken the game far too seriously and risked falling out with her friends.

Keisha was looking forward to the evening, as she would be attending choir practice. That was a relaxing time for her. As the lockdown had eased, they were now allowed to meet but still had some guidance with which to comply; some rules, such as social distancing. They could also not sing at the top of their voices, which was an advantage because some choir members tended to scream over the microphone.

Keisha was one of the lead singers in the choir. That night would be particularly exciting, as they were expecting their new choir leader to arrive. They had no idea who was taking over from Becky Telford, a bubbly Jamaican lady. The church Board of Trustees had done the interviews, but for some strange reason, never announced the name of the successful candidate.

***

Keisha drove to Abundant Life Ministries for the choir practice, which was twenty minutes away from their house. Tanya was going to spend her time with the other kids that had come with their parents. At 6:45 p.m. sharp, everyone had gathered on stage, ready to start. Then, they saw this tall man approach the stage. He looked like a basketball player, as he was in his sports gear. He towered above everyone. Keisha thought he had lost his way. But to her surprise, he proceeded to introduce himself.

"Hello, everyone. My name is Zack Armstrong. I'm your new choir conductor. I was an Assistant Choirmaster back in Atlanta for five years.

Here I am today. I'm looking forward to working with you guys. I strongly believe that our collaboration will be a fruitful one."

Keisha thought that it was funny that he should use the word 'conductor', as it sounded so old-fashioned. He explained that he was born and bred in London, but that his parents were originally from Africa and Jamaica. He was an IT consultant with a passion for gospel music. His career had taken him to America for several years, but he had been back on the shores of Britain following the pandemic. This explained why he had an interesting mixture of American and British accents. He felt it was time to come home, close to his loved ones.

He asked everyone to introduce themselves. The choir had twenty multicultural and multi-generational members. They were like a family, with ups and downs and in-fighting. But generally, everybody knew everybody, and with a few exceptions, got along just fine. Little did any one of them realise how much they would go through together in the months to come. Keisha shared how she had moved to London from the United States years before, when she came to study immunology for her Postgraduate and Master of Science degree at the Imperial College London on a scholarship, and never left. She was now working with Dexter Pharmaceuticals, a top American multinational firm.

Once everybody had shared their background and personal stories, Zack explained the vision and aspirations he had for the choir. He wanted a mixture of new gospel songs from around the world, as well as old reprises. It was obvious that some were excited at the prospect, while others were reluctant to accept the change. He asked some of the members to pray about the new vision.

Keisha wasn't really sure what to make of the new plans for the choir, but she liked the fact that he had asked the group to pray about it. It was a good start and showed that he had faith. He didn't see the choir as just a platform to entertain, but as a ministry tool, and this mattered a whole lot to her. This initial meeting with Zack lasted a little over two hours as people introduced themselves, laughed, and generally had a good time.

On her way out, he followed her. She felt self-conscious as Julie, another choir lead, was staring at them and looked displeased as they were walking toward the main door of the building. Julie often behaved as if singing for the choir was a competition and would fight to be the lead singer at special events.

"Right, you mentioned that you're from the United States," he said.

"Yes, indeed."

"Whereabouts in the States?"

"I'm from Atlanta."

"Wow, what a coincidence. I was working in the Atlanta Tech Village before relocating to London."

"That's really funny. You were living in my hometown!"

They seemed to have a lot in common. This was an intriguing encounter for both of them.

"Maybe we can discuss this over dinner sometime?"

Keisha didn't answer him. She thought he was going a little too fast for her liking. Alarm bells were ringing. She just motioned Tanya to come over to the car.

"Is this your daughter?"

"Yes, that's my daughter Tanya or Tee."

"Mum! My name is Tanya, sir."

"Hi, Tanya," he said with a friendly smile.

He seemed to be comfortable with children. "My name is Zack. How old are you?"

"Fourteen," she replied in surprise.

As Keisha watched Tanya, she noted the surprised expression on her face. *She is probably wondering why I'm introducing her, seeing as I seldomly talk to other men.* "Come on, it's time to go home; it's getting late." Keisha turned to Zack. "Tanya has school tomorrow, so we need to go. It was great to meet you."

"Bye, you two," Zack replied as they walked off.

***

Once they got home, they decided to read Tanya's favourite story in the Bible. The story of Samuel as a child. It was a special time for bonding between mother and daughter. They also said their usual evening prayers.

Suddenly, just as they were concluding their prayers, they heard a noise downstairs. Keisha instinctively asked Tanya to hide under the bed in her bedroom while she went to check out what the noise was. They were both terrified, but Keisha summoned the courage to face the potentially dangerous intruders. She had to overcome her fears. She also had to protect her child, no matter how panicked she felt. She went towards the noise and opened the curtains.

The thieves were trying to force open the large sitting room window. Taken by surprise, they fled the scene.

She called the police to report the incident but, as there had not been any break-in, there was no need for the police to come round. However, they did mention that they would increase the patrols in the neighbourhood, as apparently there had been a series of burglaries in the area.

Keisha noticed that the alarm had failed to go off during the incident. She was going to have to call their security company to report the malfunction and check what had gone wrong. They had to tighten the security around the house.

Keisha had to stay with Tanya late into the night, trying to comfort her, as she had been severely affected by the incident. They prayed together again and she seemed to calm down. "Sweet dreams, Tanya," she was whispering while playing with her daughter's hair. She then tiptoed out of the room once her daughter had fallen asleep.

Chapter II | Dealing with 'Goliath' Greg

Tanya fell into a deep sleep. She was transported into the world of little Samuel that she and her mum had read about that evening. The story takes place in Israel, centuries ago. Hannah, Samuel's mum, had cried for years because she was barren. Her rival, Peninnah, had lots of kids and used to poke fun at her. She would complain bitterly to her husband, Elkanah. He would ask her, "Am I not better than ten sons?"

One fateful day, Hannah went to the temple and met the prophet Eli. She made a vow that if God would give her a son, she would give him back to him and that no razor would ever touch his head. As she continued praying, only her lips were moving. The priest thought she'd had too much to drink. She explained that she was just sad and that she was talking to God about her situation. Eli said to her, "Go in peace; and may the God of Israel grant your request that you have asked of Him." Hannah went away, no longer sad.

God answered Hannah's prayer after many years. She had a son and gave him the name Samuel, which means *God has answered*. She decided that her son was going to serve the Lord from a young age. Elkanah also agreed. She brought him to Eli and gave him to the Lord for the rest of his life. She had kept her vow.

The boy was now living in the house of Eli – who was very old – and his wicked sons, Hophni and Phinehas. They were so evil they would steal meat from the Lord's temple. They also had lots of girlfriends! Eli tried to talk to his sons, but they would not listen. A man of God even visited Eli and told him how God was angry about what was going on. God was going to destroy the family of Eli for the sins that his sons were committing. What a terrible thing!

Samuel was different. He was an obedient boy. He was being trained under the ministry of Eli to serve God. Suddenly one night, Samuel heard a voice calling him: "Samuel!" Startled and a little afraid, he jumped out of his bed to find out who was calling him. Thinking it was Eli, he ran to him and said, "Here I am, you called me." Eli answered, "I did not call you." The boy went back to his bed.

The Lord called Samuel for the second time. Again, the boy rushed to Eli, thinking that the priest had called him. Eli responded that he had not called him. Samuel didn't know who was calling him. He had no idea that this was the voice of the Lord. He was puzzled and was wondering what was going on. If it wasn't Eli, then who was calling him?

The Lord called Samuel again a third time. On that occasion, Eli understood that it was God who was calling the boy. He said to Samuel, "Go, lie down; and when He calls you, you must say, 'Speak Lord, for your servant hears.'"

Samuel obeyed the priest's instruction. When the Lord called him this time, he repeated what Eli told him to say, "Speak Lord, for your servant hears." Then the Lord said to Samuel, "I will do something in Israel that will shock everyone. I will do what I promised against the house of Eli because he didn't get his sons to stop being naughty. No amount of offering will be able to stop me."

Just at that moment, Tanya woke up to the sound of her mother's voice. "Wakey, wakey, Tee, it's time to wake up!" She was disappointed as she was really enjoying the dream and wanted to continue the story. But her mum was shaking her real hard, so there was no way she could go back to sleep. She shared her dream with her mum and asked her, "Mum, can God speak to me the way He spoke to Samuel?" Keisha looked as if she didn't know what to answer. She managed to distract her daughter and told her to hurry up, as they both had to get on with the activities of the day.

Tanya went to her online class. There were twelve students in the class. Mrs Terrell was good to them, but strict. She would tell them off whenever they talked too much. She spoke with a very posh accent, which Tanya found interesting. The other kids liked to imitate the way she pronounced words. Greg Bell-Armstrong was a chatterbox and would interrupt the teacher constantly. She would give him extra after-school assignments because he would not listen to her.

This particular morning, he was in the mood for teasing Tanya. She had dark brown skin and bright blue eyes. Everywhere she went people would stare at her. Sometimes she felt very shy. She had been born with Waardenburg Syndrome and as a result, suffered some hearing loss. Her mother had taken her to a specialist and had found that she had Type 2 of the syndrome. She looked like a normal child, but it was unusual to see a person so dark with bright blue eyes. These were particularly striking features that children were not used to.

Greg continued the bullying, calling her names. "Tanya is a weirdo. Tanya is a weirdo. Tanya is a weirdo," Greg was chanting.

"Stop it, Greg!"

"Tanya is a freak. Tanya is an alien." He continued teasing poor Tanya.

"Stop!" She felt like crying.

She hated it and felt so uncomfortable. He liked tormenting her. This would usually happen when Mrs Terrell was busy elsewhere and could not hear him. The other classmates were laughing at her. Her closest friends, Ana and Audrey, were the only ones who came to her rescue and tried to stop him.

"Stop, Greg! You and your big nose," counterattacked Audrey, who could not stand injustice.

"Leave her alone," shouted Ana.

"Oui, arrête! Stop, Greg!" shouted Audrey even louder.

The youngster stopped, as he did not want to explain to the teacher what was going on if she ever caught them fighting. The teacher had divided them into two groups for a project. This was going on while she was busy with the other group.

At lunch break, which usually lasted forty-five minutes, Ana and Audrey joined her on their WhatsApp group.

After weeks of Greg's bullying, Tanya had had enough. She remembered the Sunday School lesson that Aunty Fifi taught them a while ago, about dealing with Goliaths. It was time for her to deal with her tormentor. She devised a plan to stop him once and for all. But she could not do it on her own. She was going to need some help. She enlisted the help of Audrey and Ana to videotape him while he misbehaved during Mrs Terrell's absence.

In the afternoon, when the teacher was away attending the other group, they set the plan in motion. As usual, he began calling her names while the other pupils laughed. The girls managed to get him on their mobile camera and then sent the clip to Tanya's phone. That evening, Tanya showed the video clip to her mother, who was understandably very upset. She promised that she would contact the school the very next day. Tanya was smiling because she knew that 'Goliath' Greg was in big trouble and that she had removed him out of the way.

***

The next morning, Greg was called by his mum while they were doing their online class. He had to leave right in the middle of it. Goliath Greg had been slingshot out of the classroom for good! They later learnt that he had been suspended for a week and that in future he would be joining the other group. The school explained to Keisha that they took the matter very seriously and had a zero-tolerance policy against bullying. Tanya and her friends were relieved; they had succeeded.

At dinnertime, both mother and daughter discussed her very unusual features. Keisha tried to reassure her daughter, but she also knew that children could be cruel to one another.

"You are beautiful, Tee, don't let anyone tell you otherwise."

"But why am I so different?"

"That's just the way God created you. You're very special, just a little bit different."

"I know that, Mum, but I'm trying to understand why."

"Well, it's like this, Tee; there are some things you can't explain."

"I get so confused sometimes, and I ask myself why I was created like this."

"Come on, finish your dinner, Tee."

"But, Mum..."

"That's enough, Tanya!"

It was also hard for Keisha because this was not the first time that her daughter's condition had brought some drama into their lives. But she wasn't ready to talk about it with anybody yet because it meant that she had to revisit the past. After supper, Keisha had some work to do, which meant that there would be no reading with her daughter that night. She had come across some documents that she wanted to review.

***

Meanwhile, Tanya was on a WhatsApp call with Audrey and Ana, recalling the look of terror on Greg's face when his mum came to call him. They could all hear the mother demanding some explanations from him, just before his session ended.

"Yes, we got him good!" exclaimed Ana. He would never try that on someone else again.

"Bien fait! Good on him!" Audrey was absolutely delighted. She felt that justice had been served.

Tanya shared the dream that she had about Samuel with her friends and they asked her lots of questions.

"Who is Samuel?" asked Ana.

"He was a prophet in the Bible. He could hear the voice of God, even as a child."

"When was this?"

"Well, a long time ago, even before the time of Jesus. He was a Jewish boy."

"Eh Bien, Tanya. I don't really believe in God. My parents say that the most important thing is to be good to people."

"I have faith in God. He is the one who showed me what to do with Greg."

"You just used your brain, c'est tout, that's all," Audrey argued.

***

After the incident, Tanya was able to focus more at school. She was much more attentive and settled. Her grades had suffered a little, but nothing that she could not recover from. The school decided to investigate further. They also offered to provide a psychological assessment and counselling. However, Keisha opted to use the Christian counsellor at their church. She had gone through some counselling years ago when things fell apart so badly in her personal life. It really helped her and she felt that it would be good for her daughter too. She had not seen the therapist for a while. They made an appointment with Mrs Kalu.

***

A few days later, Tanya went to the appointment for a psychological evaluation.

"How was your childhood?"

Tanya looked at Mrs Kalu, unsure about the question or what to answer.

"There are no right or wrong answers, Tanya. Don't be afraid. What do you remember of your childhood?"

"I don't remember much."

"Go as far back as you can and tell me what you remember."

"I don't remember a lot. Just that…"

"Yes, go on…"

"I just remember that I used to feel different."

"What do you mean?"

"Most of my friends have their father. I don't know who my father is. And Mum never wants to talk about him."

"What else do you remember about your childhood?"

"Mum used to be very sad. She used to cry a lot. She's much better now."

"How would you describe your childhood? Happy, sad, don't know?"

"At first, Mum was down all the time. She used to sit in her room in the dark. Sometimes she didn't want to get out of bed. It used to make me sad as well."

"And then what happened?"

"Then everything changed when Sharon invited us to church."

Mrs Kalu knew Sharon because they were part of the same church: Abundant Life Ministries.

"Go on, I'm listening."

"Mum was happier after that. We both gave our lives to Christ. She joined the choir. We go to church every Sunday now. Once a month we also have a ladies' group meeting."

"That's very good, Tanya. Now let's go back to when you were small. What's the earliest memory you have?"

"There was one time when Mum was too sick to get up."

"What did you do?"

"I had to call the neighbours."

"Go on…"

"Then the ambulance came."

"How did you feel?"

"I was terrified I was going to lose my mum."

"What happened then?"

"Mum had to be taken to hospital. One of her friends from school had to mind me for a few days."

"What else do you remember about your childhood?"

"Some children used to tease me a lot."

"About what?"

"About the way I look. Some kids would stare at me. Others would point their finger at me. Sometimes people would make nasty comments about my mum allowing me to put in contact lenses because they didn't believe that this was the natural colour of my eyes."

"How did you feel about that?"

"Very disturbed. I felt like the odd one out. Sometimes I feel like a sore thumb."

Tanya looked upset. Mrs Kalu tried to comfort her and give her words of encouragement.

"You're doing really great, Tanya, considering what you have gone through. Yes, you look a bit different from others. But you are a very beautiful girl. In fact, you have stunning features. Always remember that. And, sometimes people may be envious. They wish they could stand out. But they look very 'plain Jane' and want to take it out on you."

"Really… I never thought of that."

The therapist explained to Keisha that Tanya had coped rather well with the incident at school. The fact that she summoned the courage to deal with her tormentor was a testament to her resilience, strength, and faith. She was stronger than she looked. Whatever they were doing at the church was working. However, she was experiencing some anxiety concerning her appearance. She was wondering why she was different from the other kids. She also had some fears surrounding her childhood and what had happened to her mother when she had been unwell. The other issue was the absence, or lack of explanations, regarding her biological father, who and where he was. She had unanswered questions about her identity that were troubling her young mind.

Keisha admitted to her that she didn't know how to deal with the situation other than to try to reassure her daughter that everything was alright. She herself had some issues and stress surrounding her daughter's looks, but she tried very hard to hide them from her. How could she explain to her daughter about why she looked the way she did? The girl often asked her why they looked so different. She frequently tried to brush it off. However, she knew that one day she would have to answer these questions. But she felt that she needed to come to terms with her own past first. In the meantime, she would just have to manage her daughter's inquisitive mind wisely.

Later on, she suddenly remembered she had to ring the security company as they needed to beef up the security in the house. "We had an incident in our home the other day."

"Can you describe and give details of the incident so that we can log it into our system."

"Certainly. A bunch of youngsters tried to break into our house. Fortunately, I managed to scare them away."

"How did you do that?"

"I opened the curtains. They were startled by my sudden appearance and ran off."

"I see, how long has the alarm been malfunctioning?"

"I'm not sure, really. This was the first time it came to my notice."

"We are going to have to come to your residence and carry out an assessment. From the report, we will make recommendations. However, we are short-staffed due to some of our employees who have had to self-isolate. We will put you on our waiting list and as soon as we have an update, we will be in touch."

"How long do you think it will take for your visits to resume?"

"I'm not sure, Mrs Campbell. We don't know when things will get back to normal. We will keep you posted and reach out in due course."

Chapter III | The Shocking Discovery

Dexter Pharmaceuticals was a multinational manufacturer of medical drugs and vaccines. They specialised in new emerging viruses such as SARS, H1N1, and Coronavirus. Outside of the United States, the London branch was their biggest centre, with around 2000 employees. It was based in Stratford and stood like a huge campus. The laboratories were state-of-the-art and were guarded like a military facility. The security was so tight that it had taken Keisha about half an hour to get through the barrage of scanning, searching, and stamping of her employee ID card.

"Hi, Rob, you're alright?"

"Hi, Mrs Campbell, I'm okay. Can't complain as at least I still have my job." He had been working at the firm as a security officer for years.

"We're fortunate, aren't we?"

"Imagine the number of unemployed people in the hospitality industry. I don't envy them."

"I know; I thank God every day that I have a job. Most importantly, I thank Him for keeping me and my loved ones in good health."

Rob did not answer. He knew that she had a strong faith, but he was not into all of that; he did not believe in God. To him, if God existed, why would He allow all this tragedy, the pandemics, and millions of people dead? But he respected her for who she was. To him, she was a very decent woman and not a snob, unlike some of the other managers. She would always be courteous and friendly.

Keisha had spent most of her career here, and she was now in senior management. She managed a team of twenty staff. She started as a lab technician, and then moved on to become a researcher. These days, she was more involved in the managerial and regulatory side of things. Except for the lab technicians and the researchers, everyone was working from home. The question on everyone's minds was what to do with this gigantic facility. There was a conversation about selling part of it but keeping some of the offices and the labs. However, no serious action could take place with the pandemic still lingering. After all, the nation had been in shock at the announcement that the Prime Minister himself had fallen sick to the deadly virus. He had had a close brush with death, even finding himself in intensive care. This life-or-death experience had caused him to review his response towards the pandemic and to come to terms with the seriousness of the situation. What a shocker! Who would have thought? These were uncertain times. People were living in fear.

At the reception, Keisha met Laura, who had recently joined the firm.

"Hello, Mrs Campbell."

"Hi, Laura, how are you keeping?"

"I'm alright myself, but I can't say the same for my family. My aunt died of COVID-19 last month. It's been tough on the family. My mother is inconsolable, as my aunt was her only living sibling. She was still quite young."

"I'm so sorry for your loss, Laura."

"It's life, what can we say."

She thought about the pandemic and how it had forever changed their lives. So many people had lost their lives. Whole industries were at a standstill. Democracy was turned upside down as the government instructed people as to where they could go and what they could, or could not, do. Masks had to be worn in public places. Social distancing was a must in public gatherings and shops. Working from home was common. Unemployment had skyrocketed.

At her desk, she went through her emails. The place was quiet as she sat alone; her colleagues and staff had gone home. She came across an email that drew her attention. It caught her eye because the names on the email were US-based top senior executives. She instinctively knew that her name was added to the long list by mistake. Moreover, it was marked highly confidential. The internal policy of the company was that in such a case, she must not read the content or open the attachment as it wasn't addressed to her. However, for some reason, she could not resist the temptation and took a look at the documents attached.

Her heart was beating so fast. She looked around nervously. She got up and locked the door so that nobody could catch her red-handed and then began reading the email. The author was basically sending the minutes of what appeared to be a secret meeting. The attachment was the results of experiments that the firm had carried out in order to make their own vaccine against the killer disease. Dexter was slightly behind the other manufacturers, and they were desperate to catch up and get a share of the pie. Its other two major rivals, Schmid Pharmaceuticals and Macon BioPharma, had already produced a vaccine. The report attached to the email explained that there was no time to wait for conclusive tests. They would just have to get it out there and sell it to government officials, Americans and foreigners alike. The document further explained that it was a race against time. They had already lost a fair share of the market. Although testing was underway in their laboratory, the efficacy of the drug created by the firm was in doubt. They simply had not had sufficient time to do enough trials or even perfect the drug. But it was a risk they were ready to take.

Keisha was horrified. She could not believe that people could be so callous and ruthless. What was worse, was the composition of the drugs. Some of the ingredients were forbidden in the pharmaceutical world, but this seemed to have been totally ignored. The protocols for trials and tests had been bypassed. *What was the price of a human life*, she wondered. As she continued reading the document, she realised that some of the ingredients of the drugs could potentially cause infertility and even cut the lives of the patients short. This was no vaccine at all; it was nothing more than a deadly poison. They had no right to toy with people's lives like that. Moreover, they spoke of a 'human consignment' to carry out tests in their lab. This was of great concern to her. What did they mean by 'human consignment'? Were they going to use actual individuals as guinea pigs? If so, who were they and where were they coming from?

She left the office preoccupied and felt sick to her stomach. What should she do? Should she pretend she hadn't come across this report or should she whistle-blow? She was completely torn and in a dilemma. She could lose her job or worse, destroy the career she had worked so hard to build. On the other hand, the life of millions depended on the truth about the side effects of the vaccine coming out.

Keisha was absorbed, lost in her thoughts. Then suddenly, she had an idea. She would request a nine-month sabbatical as soon as she got home, just in case, to get away and avoid retaliation if she decided to go ahead and flag the incident. She could always change her mind or shorten it. It was probably the best time to do so because of the situation with the pandemic. It would also give her some time to think about what she really wanted to do with her life.

She had been with the firm for such a long time that maybe this was the season for a change. She also thought of her manager Claire. They basically tolerated each other. They were forced to work together and somehow put up with each other. She was a major source of stress and anxiety. She would get Keisha to write all her reports and prepare for her meetings, including doing the research. All Claire would do was attend executive management meetings and take credit for the hard work and effort that Keisha had put in. She would have focus group discussions and group interviews to glean vital information from them and pretend to be the sole originator of such ideas. She was fond of 'office politics' or 'office wars' – she was not quite sure what to call it – setting one clique off against another. She was also notorious for using 'snitches' and people who would 'kiss and tell' within her circles to get promoted. She had started at a level lower than Keisha a few years back, but was now her boss. Rumours had it that she slept her way to the top.

Keisha remembered a conversation she had with her a while back.

"Keisha, you need more than hard work to reach the top. Unfortunately, it's not what you know, but who you know."

"Well, I beg to differ."

"You don't get it, do you? You must have someone pull strings for you. This world is a jungle," Claire stated as a matter of fact.

Keisha tried to promote a serene atmosphere in the office. Claire had a different view and would often adopt the 'survival of the fittest' philosophy.

"I think we have to agree to disagree. I don't think Matthew is more deserving of the bonus than Ray."

"Yeah, but Ray is more useful to me in the team than Matthew."

"What do you mean? Matthew always meets his targets. He is highly skilled and competent at what he does."

She had refused to recommend Keisha for a promotion for years and would not give her the necessary feedback to develop herself. She would identify her weaknesses and use them against her. For instance, she knew that Keisha hated all the administrative tasks, such as going through all the labels to ensure the right barcode was appended. Ada would call someone like Claire an 'enemy of progress' and say that she needed to sort things out in prayer. Thinking about this made Keisha laugh out loud. She had to laugh at the situation; a cheerful heart is good medicine after all.

Keisha rushed home later that evening to attend the choir practice. She emailed the request for a sabbatical to HR. This should be a formality due to her seniority within the company.

***

The choir members had received a text that each of them was to prepare a song. They were going to sing acapella because Zack wanted to get to know each person's voice. Keisha had opted to sing You Are, a song she would put on repeat in the car or at home. The song was written by one of her favourite gospel artists. The auditions were an opportunity for some to showcase their talents, while for others it was an ordeal to watch.

Jeff tried a rap song that didn't go so well. Sarah showed that she could not sing to save her life. Uche had a beautiful voice, but picked the wrong song for the occasion. Roy's rendition was well received. Mike also gave an amazing rendition and everybody was on their feet worshipping. The highlight of the night was the performance by Olivia. It was hard to believe that this was just an audition; it looked more like a performance in the Royal Albert Hall.

Keisha's own performance was alright overall, but she knew that it wasn't her very best. Her worries had worn her down, dampening her voice. She managed to do a reasonably good job, considering her state of mind. Even she had to admit that Julie's performance was better. Julie came running out after her at the end of the auditions, sneering at her. "What happened to almighty Queen Keisha? Did you lose your sound?"

The woman had always hated her for some reason; this was an ideal opportunity to get back at her. Keisha always had the disturbing feeling that she had to watch her back when it came to Julie. She had the reputation of spreading rumours faster than Radio 1. "Well, your performance didn't come close to Olivia's, did it?" Keisha replied in a feigned innocent tone. She immediately regretted it. It was petty bickering and she loathed that; it was such a waste of time. She shouldn't have allowed Julie to draw her into this.

She just walked away to avoid any more altercations.

***

Zack later contacted her when she made it home. He informed her that she would continue being one of the lead singers. He could see that she had some solid singing skills and good technique.

"I couldn't help notice that you looked a bit nervous," he commented.

"Really?" she retorted.

"I was wondering why… There's a reason why Becky Telford chose you as one of the lead singers. She must have seen that your voice is unique and brings an interesting sound to the group. So why the sweat?"

"I'm going through some stuff at work and I'm a little worried about Tanya, that's all."

"Do you want to talk about it?"

"*Hmm*, not really, it's okay. I'm going to be alright, it's nothing serious."

She was on her guard, as she didn't know him that well. Also, this information she had could potentially lead to a big scandal, so she had to be careful whom she talked to about it. Zack mentioned that he had the difficult task of announcing to a couple of members that they could not be part of the choir any longer. It was a tough conversation to be had, but it was necessary. He was also organising more auditions to recruit singers. He had been given the responsibility of preparing the group for the Music Broadcasting Network (MBN) Gospel Choir of the Year. This was a big ask. The church needed to rise to one of its biggest challenges yet.

***

One Saturday a month was a special day for Keisha and Tanya. They would spend time in the kitchen cooking their favourite dishes in preparation for meeting a group of their friends. Keisha would teach her daughter how to cook some good old soul food. By the time the ladies and their girls showed up, the food would be almost ready.

Maëva Rakotomanana came with Alannah in tow. Adaeze 'Ada' Okeke was flanked by her twins, Nkechi and Nneka. She had a hair salon that both Keisha and Tanya visited to have their hair done. They loved dancing and were usually in charge of the music and the dance floor. They would show off the latest trends in the gospel African and international dance scene. They brought a lot of fun to the gathering. Thandiwe Dlamini and her daughter Lulama were also very quick to follow in behind them. Former work colleague, Sharon Spencer, was accompanied by Caroline. They loved all the exotic food, as sometimes the women would bring their various national dishes.

The meeting would always start with a Bible study for half an hour, followed by half an hour of prayer and worship. This particular Saturday, Sharon was leading Bible study while Ada was taking over the prayer session. They would usually pray about challenging situations. Thandiwe's husband had eloped with a young lady, twenty years younger. Ada decided that they should engage in violent prayer for the return of her straying husband. It was a scene to behold. She used all the weapons in her artillery to call back the husband and chase away the mistress.

"Bongani, come back! We call you back! May that place be too hot for you. Go back to your wife! Let the strange woman leave, we command you: that Jezebel should go and never come back!"

It was a cultural shock at first, for Maëva and Sharon in particular. They were some violent prayers. She explained to the shocked group that this was what was called 'spiritual warfare'. The dinner and the dance were a lot quieter. They danced to the tunes of some popular gospel artists from around the world.

Chapter IV | The Boy Jesus in the Temple and Pastor Ben Rescued

On Sundays, they usually went to Abundant Life. Pastor Martin Adams and his wife, Rita, had been pastoring the ministry for the last decade. They had adult children and had come to London from South Africa as missionaries. They had a fairly big ministry, with people coming from all walks of life and backgrounds. Their openness and compassion were endearing. They had overcome the scourges of apartheid.

Tanya looked forward to her Sunday School classes. Her Sunday School teacher, Aunty Fifi, would get them to dance to the Blessings on Blessings (the B.O.B. Bounce) dance right at the start to "wake them up and shake off those heavy bands" she often stated. It was a dynamic class in which there was never a dull moment. The girls were a lot quieter and more mature. Tanya, Caroline (Sharon's daughter), and Michelle (Aunty Fifi's daughter) were sometimes asked to briefly take charge of the class when Aunty Fifi or the other Sunday School teachers were busy elsewhere. Like Tanya's mum, Caroline's dad was also part of the choir. Tanya would spend a lot of time with the other two girls, although they were slightly older than she was. Destiny, Emmanuel, and Franck would constantly crack jokes and play pranks.

"Would you stop joking around, you three," said Caroline when they became too disruptive.

"Who do you think you are?" Franck replied.

"Do you want me to report you to your parents?" asked Michelle, who knew his parents and knew how afraid this would make him. He looked at her sheepishly and kept his mouth shut till the end of class, as he did not want to incur his parents' wrath.

The trio were the clowns of the group. They would often imitate those attending the church, like Deacon Peter or Aunty Fifi's husband, Assistant Pastor Kweku. Aunty Fifi found a fun way to teach them Bible stories. This week, the Sunday School teaching was based on the story of Jesus when his parents were looking for him after going to the temple in Jerusalem for the Feast of the Passover.

Destiny liked telling stories of his own. He put his hand up, wanting to share what happened to his little brother, Promise.

"Aunty Fifi, the same thing happened to my brother."

"Okay, go ahead, let's hear about it."

"My brother went out to play. He was lost for several hours and we couldn't find him. We didn't know what happened to him. My parents had to call the police. We were all so frightened; my mum was in tears. Pastor Martin prayed with us, and guess what?"

"What happened?"

"My brother was finally found. A lady tried to kidnap him." Everyone was shocked but relieved at the happy ending. Aunty Fifi managed to keep the class under control and finish the lesson.

Aunty Fifi would often do Bible quizzes or crosswords at the end of the class; she would reward the child with the most correct answers. It forced them to pay attention to the stories if they wanted to win. They would eagerly wait for the surprise gift, which invariably Benjamin or Tanya would get. They would also have arts and crafts projects that the children loved so much. Tanya and her friends felt that there was something for them and not just for the adults in the church. She liked to sit next to Benjamin or "Pastor Ben" as they called him, because he would speak like a preacher and liked to quote the Bible. There was some friendly rivalry between them both, but Ben had a greater knowledge of the gospel.

Tanya once asked him, "What do you want to be when you grow up?"

"I want to be like Apostle Paul," he replied.

"Really? Why?"

"I want to perform miracles like him. He had such a strong faith and brought so many souls to Christ," he said with an evangelistic passion.

Tanya admired his conviction. She still did not know what she wanted to be; she kept changing her mind. One minute she wanted to be an actress. Another time, she wanted to be a solicitor defending the poor or the less privileged. She sometimes thought of being a missionary among lost tribes. She envied Pastor Ben and wished she knew what life had in store for her.

Meanwhile, the adult service was very emotional. Pastor Martin had an announcement to make:

"My wife and I are grateful for the last ten years at Abundant Life. We see many of you as family. We have gone through ups and downs together. We have prayed, cried, and laughed with you. We also saw some of you marry, have children or grandchildren or go through a divorce. We have grown together. This is why we want to share something really personal with you… My wife Rita has been diagnosed with breast cancer. It's at an advanced stage. We believe in God for healing and pray for Rita to make a full recovery. We crave your prayers and understanding. I will have to step back for the foreseeable future and give Rita the support and attention she needs. I have delegated my responsibilities to Pastor Kweku, who will take over during this difficult time for my family and me. I have no doubt that he will fulfil his duties impeccably during my absence."

There was silence and disbelief. Pastor Kweku encouraged the whole church to extend their hands and pray for the pastor and his wife. Some were wiping tears off their faces.

At the end of Sunday School, the children often joined the adults.

"Why is everyone so upset? Why are people crying?"

"The pastor's wife has cancer," someone whispered.

***

Later that day, as she lay in bed, Tanya felt really sad about Mrs Pastor Rita, as she liked to call her. The pastors had always been part of her life. Pastor Martin was probably one of the few male role models in her life. When they moved into the house that her mum bought, he was there to help. When they weren't sure which car to buy, he provided much-needed advice. Sometimes he would kindly send the men from the church to do some DIY. Rita was like a grandmother to her.

She reminisced about how she would watch Rita paint her lovely paintings. Sometimes Rita would take the Sunday School class. She had a stern authority about her that made the kids respect her. Rita was also teaching her how to knit and she was so looking forward to making her first jumper. They could talk about a lot of things and Rita would answer many of the questions that her mother was too embarrassed to answer.

The other day Tanya had asked Rita what the signs were when a woman was pregnant and she patiently explained without rebuffing her. She felt at ease asking Rita about anything. She knew that there was no point going to her mum because she would fob her off. But the questions she had about her family and her own identity, even Rita could not answer.

Tanya prayed that the Lord would heal the Pastor's wife. That He would take away the cancer. She prayed fervently for a while. She then slowly fell into a deep sleep and an eventful dream.

Twelve-year-old Jesus and his family went to Jerusalem for the Passover. He had been so drawn to the temple that he completely forgot about his parents. They were a big group: some people were playing instruments and singing, kids were running around racing or playing hide-and-seek. Others were selling nice lamb kebabs and snacks of chickpeas, olives, dates, etc. Sometimes they would stop to have some food and drink hot tea. It was a noisy and joyous crowd of people.

Mary and Joseph assumed that Jesus was with some of their other relatives. They often met people from other nations and would ask questions about faraway lands. They traded and exchanged their own products for other exotic goods they had never seen before. They tried mangoes from distant Abyssinia. They would taste spices from remote Asia. They learnt of new agricultural tools from the Greek and Roman empires. It was an opportunity for people to venture into new businesses, as so many people gathered for the feast. The Passover in Jerusalem was one of the highlights of the season.

However, Jesus's parents were having a hard time and started to panic when they realised that he was nowhere to be found. They went looking for him everywhere and concluded that he must have stayed behind. This was a day's journey from Jerusalem. Mary was terrified about the fate of her child. Meanwhile, Jesus was in the temple listening to the teachers and asking them many questions. They were amazed at the boy, as he showed great wisdom in his understanding. While this was happening, his parents went combing the streets of Jerusalem, going to the market square, and the various inns and eateries. They were calling him and asking people if they had seen him. The boy seemed to have vanished.

This went on for three whole days. His parents were exhausted and worried. Where was Jesus? The last place they decided to go to was the temple. That's where they eventually located him. They were expecting to find him in a state, totally freaked out. But on the contrary, he seemed completely at ease with these strangers. Joseph and Mary were so relieved.

They had heard the horror stories of children being abducted and sold into slavery, never to be seen again.

His mother asked Him, "Son, why did you do this to us? Look, your father and I have sought you anxiously."

"Why did you seek me?" he replied. "Did you not know that I must be about My Father's business?"

They were completely stunned by his answer. They didn't have a clue what he meant by that statement. All the same, they were both relieved there was no dramatic end to their journey.

***

The next Saturday, Keisha and Tanya got together with the choir for an open-air picnic in Crystal Park, near the lake. Pastor Ben had come with them.

"Hey, guys, I wanted us to come here together to officially launch our campaign for the gospel competition. As you may already know, the leaders of the church are looking forward to us taking part in the MBN music contest coming up in a few months very much. It's an opportunity to show the stuff we're made of and somehow reach out to the world around us. It's good to leave the four walls of our church and get to know people from different communities. It could open new opportunities or ventures in the area of music ministry. We might even have our own album, who knows? Anything is possible. 'Dare to dream, dare to be different' is my motto."

"How are we going to do that?" Some were slightly sceptical about the whole thing.

"You let me worry about that. I have the roadmap for our success. We just have to follow it and we should be fine. All I require from you is that you let me know who is available. Also, please keep all this in your daily prayers."

"How long will the competition last?"

"What about the cost?"

"Can we bring our kids?"

"Hey, not everyone at the same time... we can't hear ourselves. I will send you all an email explaining all the details."

Suddenly, one of the kids came running towards the group, shouting at the top of his voice, "Mummy, Mummy, Pastor Ben is drowning. Someone pushed him in the lake!"

"What?"

Everything stopped. Then everyone went running towards the lake.

"Where did he fall?"

"Over there. He's gone under."

"We can't see; where is that?"

By the time they got to the scene where Pastor Ben had sunk, the culprits had fled. Zack, who was the most athletic, jumped into the water. After a few minutes, he came back up and went back under again. He did the same for a second time. On the third attempt, he came back with Pastor Ben's body. Zack was able to swim towards the side of the lake, but Ben's body looked lifeless. Zack tried to perform CPR on him. Someone was calling the emergency services, explaining what had happened. People started praying for him. Some, like Tanya, were crying. After what seemed like an eternity, he started breathing again.

"Where am I?" he said as he opened his eyes.

"*Shhht*, stay calm. Don't move. The ambulance is coming."

Everyone started clapping and praising the Lord. The choir members were so overjoyed and relieved. They knew that they had just avoided a tragedy. Keisha called Pastor Ben's parents. It was decided that she would go with him to the hospital. Tanya would stay behind with Zack. While they were waiting for the ambulance to come, which took a while because they had to find the exact location by the lake. Pastor Ben relayed what happened when he was unconscious.

"I saw a great light and I felt drawn to it. The more I went towards it, the lighter and better I felt. It felt so great. But then, just when I was about to reach the centre of the light, I heard a mighty voice. It said, 'Go back, it is not your time yet.' Then, I came back to my body at such a high speed. You know, just like when you're driving a sports car or a motorbike, only faster than that."

Just then, the ambulance came rushing in.

"Come on, Pastor Ben, I will follow you to the hospital," said Keisha.

Everyone was shaken by the incident. Zack decided that it was time for everyone to go home. Nobody was in the mood to talk about the competition after Pastor Ben's near-death experience.

***

At the hospital, Keisha asked Pastor Ben what happened.

"There were two boys. We were telling them about Jesus. They started teasing us. They said to me that if I have faith, I should jump into the water. I said I was not going to do that. They asked me why. And I said because I'm asthmatic. But they wouldn't take no for an answer. So, they pushed me into the lake."

"Do you know these boys?"

"No, I don't, but I could easily recognise them."

"Good, we're waiting for your parents. This will have to be reported to the police."

His parents eventually made their way to the hospital. As Keisha explained everything to them, his mum burst into tears.

"How could this happen? How can a child attempt to kill another child? This is surreal! What has this world come to?" She was hysterical.

"Calm down," her husband was trying to tell her.

"Don't tell me to calm down! They tried to kill my baby. Don't you get it?"

"He is also my son. But carrying on the way you're doing right now won't help. We've been told that his condition is stable. They will just keep him overnight and carry out the necessary tests to ensure that there are no after-effects. Let's thank God that our boy is still alive. It could have been another story."

"I know that. I'm just saying that these kids nowadays are so violent and cruel. I hope they catch them and throw them in jail. I will make sure that they face the consequences of their actions."

"Well, we're not sure who they are. We're hoping that people will come forward and they will be identified quickly," Keisha said.

Keisha understood their feelings perfectly. This was every parent's nightmare. But she was grateful that something worse had not happened and thanked God that she was not the bearer of bad news. Pastor Ben was going to be just fine!

Chapter V | Grove Park, Lewisham

Zack was smiling at the sound of the music coming from his parents' home in Grove Park, Lewisham. It was a place where he could find some peace and quiet after the hustle and bustle of city life and church politics. It was an old four-bedroom house that he would visit on a regular basis. The family had lived there since he was a child. They knew most of the other families in the cul-de-sac. He liked to visit his parents as they were always playing gospel music. His was a family of music lovers. As far back as he could remember, music was a part of them. He also liked to visit them for some sound advice when he wasn't quite sure what to do. His new role at Abundant Life Ministries had come with its challenges. He knew that they could give him some good tips about how to handle some of the issues, since his father had been a choir director in their church denomination for decades.

His twin brother, Jack, who had a family of his own and a cleaning business, visited from time to time. Jack could sing, but he was more of a football aficionado and an Arsenal supporter. He would argue passionately about football with Zack, who preferred Bukayo Saka.

"Mark my words… Watch Bukayo Saka, he is a promising player, full of talents."

"He doesn't come near Aubameyang… He is the top scorer, man. Anyway, what do you know? You've not really been following the premiership since you went to the United States."

"I've been following it a lot more since I got back. Saka is a rising star, I tell you! Anybody can see that. And the boy is only eighteen; he has the best years still ahead of him. And don't forget that Aubameyang is thirty-one."

"Well, how old are Messi and Cristiano Ronaldo?"

"Exactly my point, he is not so far behind them in age, you know."

"You're being hard! What do you know anyway? I don't know why I'm wasting my time arguing with you."

"Time will tell bro."

Zack would laugh, he did not take this too seriously, but his twin brother would make a big deal out of it.

After entering the house, he went towards the study room that they called 'the library', where the family would sing or listen to old-time greats. Zack grew up on this music. It always inspired him when he was going through a tough time. But he knew that as much as he loved it, times had moved on. The church needed a fresh and contemporary sound. He walked into the library and found his parents singing *O Peter Don't Be Afraid*. He joined them and immediately felt in his element.

His mother, Cynthia, was from Bamenda in Cameroon. She was a retired nurse. Clive, his father, was from Kingston, Jamaica, and was a doctor by profession. They had met at Lewisham Hospital, where they fell in love and then got married. They had a rocky start because Cynthia didn't come from a Christian background. She was very rough around the edges. "God had to work hard to chisel me out and make me the diamond I am today," she often said with a mischievous smile. They went through a stormy time, but they eventually worked out their differences. She grew used to some things, like not drinking or praying more than just in church on Sundays. One time, her husband caught her eating in the toilet when she was supposed to be fasting. They often laughed when they remembered those times; his patience eventually paid off.

"What's troubling you, Son?" Clive asked.

"What do you mean?"

"I know that look. What's the matter? Is it to do with work?"

Zack was silent for a moment.

"Well, work is not as exciting as it used to be, but it's not giving me sleepless nights. So much is going on. The other day a child almost drowned at a church picnic. But thankfully, he didn't. I managed to rescue him. We thank God for that."

"Thank God, I can't imagine what the parents would have felt. That was very brave of you. I'm so proud of you, Son."

"I had to do what I had to do. I was glad I was there to help. Otherwise, it would have been a real tragedy."

He was trying to downplay his role. These days, everyone was branded a hero at the slightest act of bravery. To him, it was simply natural to help someone in difficulty.

"I can very well imagine. You might even have had to cancel your participation at the gospel competition, who knows. So, it's a good thing it ended up the way it did," Cynthia, always practical, commented.

"What's really on my mind is that as the choir leader, I have to make some difficult decisions."

"Like what?"

"I have to pick the lead singer for the competition. It's a tough one because there are about two or three that could fit the bill."

"What's the problem? Just make up your mind and pick the best."

"It's not that simple. Two choir members have already come to me basically stating that they want to fill in the position."

"Who?"

"Julie and Mike. They both gave a good audition, but nothing to write home about. We need someone with a unique voice if we have any hope of making it to the end of the gospel competition. The church Board of Trustees is really counting on me. That's why they hired me in the first place."

"Are the auditions closed?" his father asked.

"Yes, a couple of weeks ago."

"Let me think... I might know someone who could be of help. His name is Jay, and he has a very special voice," said Clive. "He used to come to our church, but I haven't seen him in a while."

"Alright, I can give him an audition; we have nothing to lose. Give him my mobile number and tell him to call me if he is interested."

"See, to every problem there's a solution."

"Yes, but that's not all."

"What else?"

"I also have to choose the genres of the gospel. You know how it is; old folks want the traditional stuff, while younger generations want a more contemporary sound. The usual in-fighting."

"Well, what does the Pastor prefer?"

"I'm not sure. I haven't really been able to discuss it with him. He is going through a difficult time."

"What's the matter?"

"He announced last Sunday that his wife was diagnosed with cancer."

"My, my, my, that's a tough one."

"I want us to sing contemporary songs from around the world."

"Jay might just be the right guy then. He is quite eclectic with his music and can sing different genres of gospel. He is an interesting guy and he writes his own songs too."

"Wow, that's awesome!"

"You sound so American when you say that," said his father, laughing.

Many of his friends had also said that to him since he arrived back from Atlanta.

"Yeah, but it's true, though. Not every lead singer can write their own songs; that's pretty special." He felt so much better and relieved after talking to his parents. That's why he missed Grove Park and that's what made him come back again and again. There was indeed no place like home.

He went into the kitchen to have a little chat with his mum and eat some tasty Jamaican food: goat curry with rice and peas. He knew immediately what his mum was going to talk about.

"What about... what's her name again? I spoke to her one time on WhatsApp..."

"Joyce, you mean? I told you it was over between us a long time ago, Mum."

"She sounded nice though. I thought you would have settled down with her by now."

"Well, it didn't work out between us. We just drifted apart, that's all."

"That's a shame. And in your new church, is there anyone who has caught your eye?" Cynthia asked.

"Mum!"

He thought about the choir and the church in general. It was always the same story: single ladies looking for someone to marry, predators looking for someone to go out with and abuse, married men having affairs, and business people trying to sell something and make money.

In the choir, he was the centre of attention for several ladies. Julie was the most aggressive, which really put him off. She would constantly come and ask him if he needed help with something. She acted as if they were together already. It got on his nerves because it gave out the wrong impression. He had no interest in or attraction towards her. Also, she had tried using her charms to get the lead singer role, and that was so unethical to him. In fact, he was totally disgusted by her behaviour.

"What?!? I'm just asking… You might meet a good woman."

"I'm too busy for that."

"Really? Are you sure?"

As Zack watched the emotions flick across her face, he realised she knew something more was going on. Being very intuitive, she probably understood that he was not just worried about things at church. Zack couldn't hide his feelings from his mum. He decided to seek her opinion. Maybe, being a woman, she could help.

"There's a lady in the choir," he admitted. "She's a strong Christian and attractive as well. But she's so reserved and introverted."

"What's her name?"

"Keisha Campbell and her daughter's name is Tanya."

"Oh, she has a daughter? How old is she?"

"She is fourteen."

"Interesting…"

"Yeah… I try to get closer to her, but each time she shuts me down."

"Why don't you invite her out somewhere?"

"We're really limited with the lockdown at the moment, you know."

"You're going to have to come up with a brilliant idea, Son. Better still, ask God," she said with a wink.

"I do need God's intervention," he replied, smiling.

***

The next morning, Zack went to work. He was having a hard time. Not because he did not like his job, but because he felt torn between his job and his choir activities. He needed time to prepare the songs, the music, and to harmonise the vocals. That morning he had a one-to-one meeting with his manager James (Jim) Latimer.

"What do you think of the new project coming up?"

"It's good for the firm."

"You don't sound too thrilled. Is anything the matter?"

"No, not really."

"I was going to put your name forward to manage the project."

"Oh, really?"

"Well, I think you have the two things we're looking for: the expertise and the experience. I think you did something similar when you were in the United States, didn't you?"

"Correct."

"So, this should be no problem for you."

Zack felt conflicted. On the one hand, he didn't want to disappoint his boss. On the other hand, he had his choir leader commitments outside of work, which was (for him) top priority. He did not know what to say to Jim. He had worked with him since he had come back from the States and they had come to respect each other. Jim came from a working-class background and worked hard to rise through the ranks, which was a testament to his determination and perseverance. Behind his simple demeanour and his Cockney accent, he was smart; make no mistake. He worked well with Zack. He very quickly spotted his talents and identified his strengths. This is the reason why Zack felt so bad. He did not want to let down the man who had banked on him.

"You don't seem too excited by all this. This could be the break that you've been waiting for."

"I'm just trying to achieve a work-life balance. I have some commitments outside of work that are keeping me very busy."

"You also need to make time for work if you have any hope of getting your bonus and a promotion at the end of the year. Anyway, I want you to go and think about all this. I need to know by next week."

"Okay, I'll think about it."

"I do hope that you make the right choice, Zack. Opportunities like these don't come knocking very often. So, tread carefully."

"I'll have a think and I'll let you know."

Zack needed time to process things. The prospect of a promotion and a very alluring £10,000 bonus at the end of the year was extremely tempting. As a young man, he was very ambitious and he would have jumped at the offer. But he was not feeling the same about the job anymore. Now he was more mature, and less ambitious or 'hungry' as Jim would put it. He wanted something more in life. He needed to get his priorities right. It was about time for him to settle down. He wanted a family of his own.

Keisha came to mind. He had not been able to get her out of his mind. He thought she could be the one. He had had some relationships in the past, but she had left him with strong feelings and he thought about her often. She was very attractive, with an average height and build; not too big, but not too skinny. She had the right curves in the right places, just the way he liked it. He knew that she was a clever and wise woman. He liked to talk to her. But he particularly liked the fact that she had faith in God; something that had been missing in most of the women in his life. She was different. However, he wondered what happened to her for her to be so stand-offish. He suspected that she might have gone through some kind of painful experience in the past that had caused her to be so wary of men. He was going to do everything in his power to turn her attitude around. There had to be a way to win her over.

He was also thinking about ministry. He wanted to channel his energy towards the work of God. He knew in his heart that a new IT project was not part of his plans. It was not something he was looking forward to. He had to find a way to get through to his boss. But that would be for another day.

***

At the choir rehearsal, Zack was to announce who was going to sing the main parts.

"Guys, you know that we were on the lookout for a lead singer for the competition and have some very talented singers in our midst. We are truly blessed to have you all in this church. And every Sunday you do your best to minister in song to the congregation. We really appreciate this."

Everyone was waiting in anticipation to know who would be selected.

"However, I think it's important to go with the very best and strive for excellence as we are going to compete with some of the best choirs in the country. So, that's why I have chosen someone whom I think will fill this role perfectly, and I think that you will agree with me. Let me introduce you to Jay. He will sing a couple of songs for us. He has a strong and unique voice. Let's hear him."

Jay gave an amazing performance and had a special voice that stood out. Almost everyone was happy about the selection, except Julie.

***

At home, Keisha and her daughter held Bible study before going to bed. Tanya was very focused during Bible study time, paying attention to every detail and asking many questions. They read the story of the five loaves of bread and the two fish in the book of Matthew, chapter 14.

"The disciples came to Jesus asking him to send the crowd away so that they could go to the village and buy themselves some food."

"Oh, oh, they were thinking about themselves."

"Let's not judge so quickly. The Bible says that there were five thousand men, besides women and children. Imagine having to feed all of them."

"Oops, I hadn't thought of that, actually."

"Imagine all those kids witnessing the miracle of multiplying the bread and the fish for all to eat. Always remember that God is the God of miracles. Nothing is impossible for Him. He can provide all your needs, as was the case in this story. The disciples and the crowd were hungry. Jesus fed them with the little there was and multiplied it. He is the God of multiplication. Because the crowd followed Jesus, they did not lack food and did not go hungry. That's the kind of God we serve."

"That's amazing, Mum!"

"We serve an amazing God. Just like those kids, you can also experience the miracle of God."

They then took time to pray, especially for the homeless kids who did not have a place to call home, or food to eat, so that the Lord would provide for them.

"Right, let's go to bed. Sweet dreams, Tanya."

"Good night, Mum," she responded and gave her mum kisses and a hug.

Chapter VI | Raising the Alarm

Back in the office, Keisha could not sit still. She was anxious, wondering what the repercussions would be. She was tapping nervously on her desk and felt sick to her stomach. She knew that what she was about to do could put her life in danger, as so much was at stake. But she had made up her mind that this was the right thing to do. Besides, HR had granted her sabbatical request, so today was her last day. She had endured many sleepless nights over the past few weeks. Her conscience would not let her be.

At precisely ten o'clock, she picked up the phone, dialled the whistleblowing line, and made a report. She explained everything she had found out about the vaccine – its illegal ingredients and potentially deadly side effects.

Unbeknown to her, the call was recorded and automatically transmitted to the executive management of the firm. In Dexter's, whistleblowing was divided into codes: green, amber, and red. Green was considered not too serious, and would not affect the firm. Amber was mildly serious and may require management intervention, although this was highly unlikely. Red was considered extremely serious and warranted the intervention of a senior executive of the firm because it might cause serious financial and reputational damage. Keisha's whistle blowing was deemed to be a 'code red'. The call was anonymous, but only to a certain extent; it was easily traceable. Someone high up heard the entirety of the call and contacted Keisha's boss, Claire McPherson.

Keisha went past her office to go to the toilets when she overheard her name.

"Keisha did *what*?!?" Claire was screaming, which was very unlike her, so she stopped in her tracks to listen to what was being said. She became acutely aware that her whistleblowing exercise had not remained confidential and anonymous, as was stated in the internal policy of the firm. She was disgusted, as this was totally unacceptable. It was a complete breach of trust and confidentiality.

"Don't worry, I'm going to take care of this… We've got to get rid of her very fast before this gets out. But we need a clean job…"

Just then, Keisha's mobile phone rang. She was horrified. This was the worst time for this to happen. Claire turned around to see who was there, but couldn't see anybody. Keisha had managed to escape by ducking past her desk. She crawled until she was out of sight. Then, she ran back to her office and was shaking. Her heart was pounding. That was a close call! She checked her phone. It showed a missed call from Pearl, who usually looked after Tanya when she had commitments.

And right at that moment, Claire walked into her office.

"Were you looking for me just now?" she asked.

Keisha answered innocently, "No, I wasn't, why do you ask?" She tried to sound normal.

"You're sure? I could bet my money that I heard someone by my office…"

"Yes, actually. I'm on my way out." Keisha was trying to get away from her as fast as possible. The atmosphere in the room was electrifying. One could almost feel the negative vibes.

"Alright," Claire replied, but she looked unconvinced. "I will talk to you later," she said. She sounded threatening. And then she walked out of the room.

Keisha held her heart for a moment, trying to recoup and calm down. Her hands were all sweaty and shaking. She managed to control herself enough to ring Pearl back.

"Keisha, you need to come back home. Tanya is not feeling well."

"What's wrong with her?"

"It might be some bug or something. She's out of sorts. I've given her some paracetamol. She's sleeping now."

"Give me about an hour and a half."

"Okay, I'll see you then."

Keisha put her affairs and her desk in order. She left Dexter's, unaware that she had set in motion a chain of events that would turn her quiet life upside down. She was also unaware, totally lost in her thoughts, that she was being followed. She was constantly reliving the moment she heard Claire in the office. *We've got to get rid of her.* Her manager's words kept ringing in her ears like a leitmotif. There was no doubt that her life was in danger. She was worried about her safety, but most importantly, the safety of her daughter. She needed to act fast. It would not take her too long to realise that they were already after her.

***

Keisha rushed into her three-bedroom house, situated in Finsbury Park. It would generally take her twenty minutes by car (without traffic) to get from her workplace in Stratford to the doorsteps of her home. When the traffic was heavier, it could take her as long as an hour. It was a busy but safe neighbourhood, and she had purchased the house when houses in London were not yet outrageously expensive and she could afford to buy. Nowadays, a similar house in the area could set one back eight or nine hundred thousand pounds minimum, due to its proximity to London. The house boasted two bathrooms, which she really wanted. But what she was most proud of was the walk-in closet where she stored her collections of dresses, bags, and shoes.

Tanya liked to go into the closet and read. Sometimes she would put on her mother's shoes and play with her bags. One day, when she was about five years old, she gave Keisha such a fright. She had looked for Tanya everywhere and thought that someone had kidnapped her. Tanya had fallen asleep in the walk-in closet. Thankfully, Keisha managed to find her before she called the police.

"What's wrong with Tanya?" she said in a loud voice.

"Shhhh," Pearl whispered, putting her finger on her lips. "She is still sleeping."

"What happened? She was fine when I left her earlier on."

"She started complaining of headaches and actually got sick. When I checked her temperature, she was quite hot and seemed feverish. That's why I thought I should give you a shout. I think she's coming down with some bug or something. I think the sleep is helping."

"Okay, we'll let her be for the time being."

"Let's go to the kitchen. I have some tea prepared," Pearl suggested.

"Yeah, I need that right now. I think you should stay for the night; you can have the guest room. I have a nightie for you."

"Sounds like a plan."

"I think Tanya hasn't been well since the incident with Pastor Ben."

"Who is Pastor Ben? And what happened?"

"You know, he's Tanya's friend in the Sunday School. They're always together. She talks about him quite a lot. Did she not tell you what happened to him?"

"No, she didn't mention anything. Besides, she was not a hundred per cent, remember? She wasn't really talking that much today."

"He almost drowned the other day."

"How come?"

"We went with the choir to the park. One of the lads pushed Pastor Ben into the lake. Now, the thing is that he is asthmatic. So, he had an attack right in the water."

"Oh, my lord! That's awful! Did they catch the boys?"

"Yes. Someone videoed them on their mobile phone and handed it in to the police."

"Are they going to press charges?"

"Can you believe it, Pastor Ben asked them not to press charges, but he asked for a special request."

"What was that?"

"That they attend a weekly session at our church for a year."

"Wow, what a forgiving heart he has. He is so good."

"He is a true Christian."

"You can say that again."

"Did they agree?"

"You bet they did! Who would want to risk going to a juvenile or young offenders' institution?"

"Now I see what you mean by Tanya being affected. She must have been in a state."

"She was terrified. She thought she had lost her friend. It was a horrible experience. And I think it did affect her in some way. Maybe that is why she is not a hundred per cent."

The two women were now more relaxed, chatting away. Pearl was the English version of her Filipino name Perla. She was an aspiring actress who had been doing childminding to supplement her income. She had come over to the United Kingdom in the hope of making it big as a screen actress or movie star. So far, her big breakthrough had eluded her. But maybe someday she would receive the call that she had been waiting for forever. She was a staunch Catholic and always lit a candle at church and prayed that God would answer her.

After helping Pearl set up for the night, Keisha went to Tanya's room, kissed her on the cheek, and whispered her usual, "Sweet dreams, Tee."

What she did not know, was that Tanya was indeed having one of her dreams.

This time, it depicted the story of Elisha and the widow's oil. She was the wife of a prophet who had died. They had nothing and were very poor. She was in a state of panic and did not know what else to do to raise the money they owed and take care of her family. She went to the Prophet Elisha crying out to him: "Prophet Elisha, the person I owe money to is coming after me. He is getting ready to take my two sons as slaves."

"What shall I do for you? Tell me, what do you have in the house?"

"We have nothing but a jar of oil."

"Go and borrow big clay containers from everywhere, from all your neighbours; do not get just a few. Then, when you come in, shut the door behind you and your sons, then pour oil into all those vessels, and set aside the full ones."

She left him and shut the door behind her and her sons, who brought the big containers. She filled all the containers and said to one of her sons: "Bring me another one of those containers."

"There are none left," he answered.

The whole house was filled with containers and there was no room left. The oil stopped flowing because there were no more containers available. She went back to the Prophet Elisha and told him what had happened.

He said to her: "Go and sell the oil and pay your debts. You and your sons live on the rest."

Tanya could still see the image of all the clay containers in the house while her mum was shaking her frantically.

"Tanya, wake up," she was whispering. "Let's go. Take your shoes and let's go."

She grabbed Tanya, who was still weak but felt a little better. She was confused why they were in the dark and leaving the house in a hurry.

"Why, Mum, what's up?"

"There's no time now… I will explain later, let's just go."

"Where is Pearl?" asked her daughter.

"There's no time for questions right now, Tanya."

They left the house through the patio door, walked down the side path, and got into the car. Keisha barely had the time to grab a small bag that she kept ready in the walk-in closet in case of emergencies. She decided to drive to the church, which was situated in Whitechapel, as she had the keys that Pastor Martin had given her. The building was large and had various activity rooms for prayer, Bible classes, and offices.

***

When they reached the building, they went towards the room where the church sometimes held retreats. That's when they bumped into someone.

"Who is this?" asked Keisha in a frightened voice. Tanya's heart skipped a beat.

"It's me, Zack."

"Oh, what are you doing here at this time of the night?"

"And what are you two doing here at this time? It's almost midnight."

"It's a long story. But first, I've got to use my mobile phone."

She took her phone and went into one of the rooms, leaving Tanya with Zack.

"Are you alright, Tanya?" Zack asked, slightly worried.

"A bit weak and tired. Not too well, to be honest."

"Have a seat. You poor thing. Where did you guys come here from?"

"From home."

"Why did you come to church so late?"

"I don't know, Mum didn't tell me."

"Oh, I see."

"What are you doing in the church so late?" she found the strength to ask.

"I was doing some work for the choir."

Meanwhile, Keisha was still shaking, and these few minutes gave her a little time to try to compose herself. She hoped that neither had noticed how distraught she was. She didn't want to call the police because she needed time to think. She was grateful that crimes could be reported online in her area; the process having gone digital a couple of months before. The pandemic had sped things up as, due to the lockdown, people were encouraged to stay home rather than visit the police station. She filled in an online form to report that someone had sustained a fatal injury at 7 Wilberforce Road, Finsbury Park. It might take a while for the police to respond. She was still a little shaky. She did not want Tanya to know what had transpired that night.

"You guys can't stay here, it's too cold," said Zack.

Keisha jumped when he came into the room. She was so nervous after what had occurred back at home.

"Tanya told me she isn't feeling well," he added.

"I know. But we have no choice right now, we left in a hurry. This was not planned."

"You can stay at my place. It's more cosy there than here. You guys need a proper bed to sleep in."

"That's true, Mum. I'm knackered."

She could see that her daughter looked exhausted, so decided to accept Zack's offer. She felt so overwhelmed. The events of the past few hours had had a huge impact on her, and she needed to recover from the shock. She also needed time to think about what her next move was going to be.

They left the church and followed Zack's car in theirs.

***

When they got to Zack's place, in the befittingly called area of Gospel Oak on Shirlock Road, Tanya went straight to bed.

"Would you like some tea, Keisha?"

"Yes, please. What were you doing at the church so late?"

"Just some housekeeping for the choir."

"Like what?" She was trying to avoid talking about the recent events.

"Like where to put the sopranos, altos, etc. You know; the usual conundrums. I have selected almost all the songs that we are going to sing. I just have to check with the pastors that it's okay. So, I had to send them an email as well. I also had to speak to the organisers of the MBN gospel competition… You know, just to touch base with them. We have to coordinate and liaise about the hotel, bookings, transportation, etc."

"I see."

"What about you guys?"

"It's a very long story that I'm too tired to tell right now. Can we save it for tomorrow?"

"Alright, okay. Let me show you to your room."

While in bed, she broke down and cried. She was still haunted by Claire's words: *We've got to get rid of her.* She was also thinking of the poor innocent Pearl who had died in her house. Pearl's life had come to an abrupt end. Her dream of becoming an actress would never materialise. Keisha remembered the number of times Pearl was in tears because an audition did not go well. Or the times when she was so depressed because she was not selected for a part she had so wanted.

Keisha felt so guilty because she knew that the young woman wasn't the target; that she was the one meant to have been killed that night. What did they call it again? Survivor's syndrome? Or was it survivor's guilt? It was something to that effect. She remembered seeing a documentary on one of the satellite channels about it years ago. It was the story of a 911 survivor who felt guilty, having escaped death, while his wife and children lost their lives.

She had to find a way to keep all this from Tanya. She had already had a shock with the incident involving Pastor Ben. She feared that it would be too much if she told her the truth about Pearl's fate. She said a prayer and then fell asleep.

She woke up several times during the night dreaming of Pearl and Charlie and shouting, "No, Charlie!"

She was covered in sweat. She hadn't had such dreams in years. The psychotherapy she had gone through had helped, but the events of the last twenty-four hours seemed to have triggered the nightmares once again.

Chapter VII | Confronting the Past

In the morning, after praying, she had a quick shower in the guest room. It was a three-bedroom house that Zack had bought while he was working in the States. It was conveniently located a reasonable distance from the church, which is why he was able to work late. He was preparing for the choir's competition rehearsal. Situated between Kentish Town, Hampstead, and Camden, the duplex was a little gem. He had been fortunate enough to buy it at a reasonable price during the 2008 recession and never looked back. It had a rear courtyard where he liked to have barbecues.

Zack could not be happier that he and Keisha were together. He couldn't get her out of his mind. There was something about her that drew him to her. He had tried several times to get closer, but she always kept her distance. Maybe this was the opportunity he needed to get to know her better. He had so many questions that he hoped she would answer rather than pushing him away, as was her habit.

Meanwhile, Keisha could not help thinking about Pearl. She remembered the times she would come and mind Tanya and her friends. Tanya would tell her stories of how they would play pranks on Pearl. While she was having a little nap after a night of partying, they would come and tickle her feet or put an object up her nose. She would wake up and scream: "Tanya, don't let me catch you!" The girls would run off laughing. Sometimes, when Pearl would take her bath, they would hide her towel and her clothes. Other times they would switch off the hot water, and she would have to come out of the shower covered in shower gel because the water was freezing cold! They found it all so hilarious. Even Keisha found it hard to keep a straight face while scolding Tanya and her friends when she returned home. They would miss Pearl dearly. She promised herself that the killer would be found and brought to justice; she owed it to Pearl.

Her mind then turned to Charlie. She hoped that the nightmares would not come back to torment her. She had put the tragedy that struck them so many years ago behind her once and for all. She had managed to put the pieces of her shattered life back together, or so she thought.

"Keisha, breakfast is ready. Come over to the kitchen."

"I checked on Tanya. She's still asleep, but at least her fever has gone. I might take her some tea and toast later," she explained.

"Yeah, I agree. It's better to let her have a good rest."

When they sat at the breakfast table, he asked: "So, what happened last night? Why did you find yourselves in the church so late?"

"Something terrible happened, but I don't want Tanya to find out yet. She would be traumatised."

"What happened?"

"Pearl, my childminder, was killed last night."

"How?!?" He opened his eyes and mouth wide in shock. "How did it happen?"

"I think they wanted to kill me instead of Pearl."

"Did the alarm not go off?"

"No, that's the thing… We had an incident recently where some thugs were trying to break into our home. Our alarm malfunctioned."

"That's not good, is it? An alarm could have prevented her death."

"I know. It's terrible, isn't it? The security company didn't have enough staff and could not send anyone straightaway. They've advised us that they will be visiting soon. But now, nobody will be able to go there pending the investigation."

"How do you know she's dead?"

"I saw a man strangle her just outside the bathroom. She had just been to the toilet. He didn't see me, but I saw him. He left quickly. I went to check on Pearl, but she was dead. Once I was sure he was gone, I woke Tanya up and we fled. I'm sure he meant to kill me, not Pearl."

"How do you know for sure?"

"I discovered something at work."

"What did you discover?"

"Something that could bring the entire firm down. I mean, it could shut it down for good. Unfortunately for me, they found out that I know their secret. I overheard my boss saying they should get rid of me. And now Pearl is dead. It's a case of mistaken identity."

"That's terrible."

"The vaccine they produced has not properly been trialled and could potentially be harmful to humans."

"You don't mean it!"

"I tell you, I'm as shocked as you are. There is even more."

"What?"

"I read about some 'human consignment'."

"And what's that all about?"

"That's the thing... I'm not entirely sure, but... it's getting me really worried. I can only second guess. I suspect that they will use people as guinea pigs for their experiments. The question is, who are they going to use for their tests? Where are they from? All of this is illegal, by the way. They have to follow a certain protocol for clinical research, but I won't get into the technicalities with you. You see, there's what you call the Declaration of Helsinki by the World Medical Association. It sets the ethical standards for medical research involving humans. From what I read in that document, I can safely conclude that the experimental protocol has not been clearly formulated and respected. For instance, I'm not aware of any scientific literature or animal experimentation upon which Dexter's research has been based."

"Who knows? Maybe they have done all of that, but have kept it under wraps?"

"That's what worries me. It's not usually done like that. Normally, they would keep us posted about the latest developments. I have worked in this pharmaceutical firm for over twelve years now and that's how it's always been. We pride ourselves on setting the standards within the industry. This time round, it's been different. I have not heard or seen anything in relation to this vaccine. Even if there was a protocol, I'm not aware that it has been approved by an independent ethics committee, which is best practice. Also, there's been no mention of the monitoring of ongoing trials. We have not been kept in the loop about any serious adverse events. All of these are red flags to me... In my opinion, the experimental protocol has not been duly followed. Sorry, I get passionate about these things and can go on and on. In a nutshell, the research might not have been carried out ethically. I'm also in doubt as to the quality and the efficacy of the vaccine."

"That's pretty shocking. What did you do with all that information? 'Cause they need to be held accountable. They need to be answerable to someone."

"I actually blew the whistle at my firm. It was supposed to be confidential and anonymous, but I overheard my boss talking about me shortly after I made the call. I'm pretty sure that she's aware of what I did."

"They shouldn't find out that you're still alive or else they will come after you to finish the job. At least you're safe here. I wouldn't go back to your home right now. Did you report it to the police?"

"I think you're totally right. I shouldn't go anywhere near my house at the moment. I don't want to alert the people who masterminded this. I feel like I'm fighting against a whole system and that there has been a systemic cover-up. I feel somehow all alone. I did fill in the police form online and I'm just waiting for the police to get back to me."

"You're not alone. I'm here to support you, Keisha. I'm on your side. In any event, you did the right thing; lives are at stake, you know. It's very brave of you to stand up for what is right."

"Thank you so much."

She was grateful that he didn't think that her story was far-fetched. Keisha went to attend to Tanya. She was relieved that her daughter had just had a dream and was keen to share it with her. This was a welcome distraction, and she would hopefully not ask anything about what had happened the night before.

***

Zack watched Keisha walk off and felt really impressed and admired her for her stance. He could tell that she was an educated and highly intelligent woman. She had done alright for herself. Moreover, she had a good work ethic. He truly believed that this was the right woman for him, but it was not the time to say a word to her. He silently smiled, thinking that God had truly intervened to bring them closer. The fact she was even going to stay at his place far exceeded his expectations.

However, Zack was seriously worried. This was a case of murder and he was now involved first-hand. After getting lost in deep thoughts, he decided to call his office and take some time off.

***

"Mum, I dreamt of Joseph. You know, when he was seventeen."

"Oh yeah, that's in Genesis 37, where he has two dreams. One in which his siblings' sheaves bowed before Joseph's sheaf. In the second dream, the sun, the moon, and the eleven stars bowed before him."

"Yes, and Joseph's brothers became so jealous that they tried to kill him. It was so scary in the dream. And then, Reuben rescued him from the other brothers. He convinced them to throw Joseph in the pit instead. But Judah got his brothers to sell Joseph to some foreigners; I can't remember their names now. Joseph was sold and taken to Egypt."

"That's right; the brothers then pretended that Joseph had been killed by smearing his tunic with animal blood. Jacob, their father, was inconsolable. He could not believe his son had died. What the brothers did was horrible, but there was a happy ending to this story."

Keisha was trying to distract Tanya for as long as possible.

"I think I remember how the story ends, Mum. Years later, Joseph comes back into their lives, giving them food so that they will not starve to death."

"Correct. He had become very rich and powerful in Egypt. The dreams he had as a teenager actually came to pass in the most unexpected way. The lesson is that no matter how much they tried to stop what God had planned, it still happened. What was meant to be, was meant to be," said Keisha philosophically.

"Wow, isn't that amazing, Mum? I wish I had dreams like that, that come to pass in real life. I wish to have a dream that I'm a famous star, beautiful and rich, and that it then comes true."

"Oh well, at least you have dreams. Some people never dream. It makes the stories in Bible so real to you. It's a gift."

"It's true. I never thought of it like that, Mum." Tanya became wrapped up in her thoughts.

In the afternoon, they both went for a nap in their respective rooms. Suddenly, Keisha woke up screaming: "Pearl, Charlie, no!" Zack could hear it from the sitting room where he was working on the songs for the choir competition. He rushed to the room where Keisha was sleeping. She was shaking and covered in sweat. Her long natural afro hair was all over the place.

"Keisha, wake up, it's just a nightmare! Hey, wake up!"

"Hmm, what's going on? What are you doing here?" She was completely disorientated.

"You just had a nightmare."

"Pearl, Charlie…" she whispered.

"Who is Charlie?"

She just stared at him, looking completely down. The recent incident at her place was really taking a toll on her mental health.

"Look, I'm going downstairs. We can sit in the courtyard, it's secluded, that way we won't disturb Tanya."

Keisha joined Zack in the courtyard. It was a quiet and glorious day. She could smell the scent of the flowers all over the courtyard. She sipped the peppermint tea that Zack had made her.

"Who is this Charlie?" asked Zack. "Last night I also heard you screaming his name, but by the time I checked on you, you had gone back to sleep."

She felt she needed to talk. She needed to share what was tormenting her.

"Charlie was my first child. I had him with my ex-husband Felix before Tanya was born."

"Where is he?"

She stayed silent for a while. Painful memories came rushing back. It was one of the most traumatic experiences she had ever gone through.

"I... I killed him," she whispered, tears streaming down her face.

Zack was speechless. This was the second time that death was mentioned. He did not know what to make of it. This was one of the most eventful days he had experienced in the longest while.

"I had rushed out of the house after an argument with Felix, but I didn't know that Charlie had followed me. I came out of the driveway so fast that the impact killed him instantly. By the time I realised what had happened, it was too late. I had just killed my little boy. It was the worst day of my life."

She was now crying uncontrollably.

"I'm so sorry, Keisha." He was stroking her gently on the back, trying to comfort her. "I can't imagine what you must have felt. Let's pray, Keisha. The Lord will help you get over this. He will remove the grief and the pain from you."

She was pleasantly surprised that he was this spiritual. She was deeply touched that he would even consider praying for her situation. She could see how caring he was and had truthfully not expected this. To her, he looked like a womaniser or a playboy. This was so far from the truth. She was starting to like him. As they prayed together, she could feel the peace engulfing her, and was able to calm down.

As she went down memory lane, she remembered the argument she had with her ex as if it was yesterday, even though over a decade had passed. He had accused her of infidelity. Tanya was born with blue eyes.

Tanya's father was part of the Tikar, a tribe from North West Cameroon and his mother was a Fulani from Nigeria. He was absolutely convinced that there was no way that their daughter could be born with eyes that colour and that his wife had had an affair with another man. All attempts to deny the accusations and prove that he was wrong fell on deaf ears. It was during one of these arguments that the tragedy happened. Their marriage never recovered. Soon afterwards, he had asked for a divorce and was never seen again.

"I had just given birth to Tanya when this happened. That's the reason why Tanya has my maiden name instead of Kimi, her father's surname. He used to tell me that he came from the Tikar kingdom of Ngambe."

"What a coincidence; my mother is in fact from Cameroon. I've heard about the Tikar. In the States, there's a strong movement of people discovering their ancestry. I think Condoleezza Rice and Quincy Jones are Tikar descents. Does Oprah Winfrey not also have Tikar ancestry?"

"I'm not quite sure… I saw a YouTube programme called Genealogy that notable people such as Spike Lee, Vanessa Williams, and Don Cheadle were able to trace their ancestry to the Tikar."

"Why did you not do a DNA test?"

"I felt that he should believe me. He should trust me. I knew that I hadn't cheated on him. I also heard of black couples with white children, but it didn't break up their marriages. They trusted their wives. Our marriage broke down, which means that it wasn't rock solid. I went through postnatal depression and had to undergo counselling and therapy for years. My faith did help me tremendously to overcome my son's death, the divorce, the depression, and being a single mother. I had moved away from the Lord, though I must confess I was really just a nominal Christian prior to the tragedy. I rededicated my life to Him."

Sharon Spencer, who had also worked at Dexter's, had introduced her to the Abundant Life Ministries. The Canadian had since moved into a different role with another pharmaceutical company.

Just then, her mobile phone rang. It was the police calling her, following up on the online form she had filled in the night before. She was to do a Zoom call the next morning to answer some questions that the detective inspector in charge of the murder case had. She was sent the details of the call by email.

Chapter VIII | Ada's Hair Studio

At nine o'clock sharp, Keisha was on a Zoom call talking to Detective Inspector Brian Hunt. He had striking ginger hair and looked down at her with his glasses on his nose. Detective Hunt seemed very detached and cynical, acting as if this was just another murder case among many. This was an unpleasant meeting for her. She was expecting more sympathy, more compassion from him. Keisha's heart was aching for Pearl. She wanted to see justice done, but for now, she had to play safe and lie low or run the risk of being hunted down by the killer. The detective was obviously in a hurry to close the meeting. He mentioned that her home had been cordoned off, and that nobody was allowed to enter the scene of the crime pending the investigation. She was also asked not to leave the country. She provided Zack's address as her current place of residence.

"Do you think the murderer will ever be caught?" she asked Detective Hunt.

"Hard to tell, but this is a rather difficult case, as we have no leads. Nobody seems to have seen anything, apart from you. It's still early days. We don't have a suspect or a motive yet. Also, the killer is at least thirty-six hours ahead of us. The victim was not even in her own house at the time of the attack. We have been in touch with her loved ones, who have been advised of her fate and we have made arrangements to do some questioning. Because of the recent lockdown, we have to conduct these interviews over Zoom, which is new for us in the force. When we interview face-to-face, it's easier to capture the reactions and facial expressions of the people we interview; this is often crucial in our enquiries. It's a hard case to crack by the looks of things, but you never know. We may still receive a tip or a piece of information that may help resolve the case. Only time will tell."

Keisha felt discouraged by the detective's explanations. Would they ever catch the assassins? She had not dared tell Detective Hunt about what had transpired at the office with Claire. She did not trust this detective and felt that talking too much could land them in even more trouble. But she also knew that this was a vital piece of information that she was withholding, so she could not entirely blame the police for not making progress, could she?

***

A few days later, Keisha and Tanya had an appointment at Ada's Hair Studio. The shop had just recently opened, following the ease of the lockdown. It was time to get their hair done.

It was especially busy since nobody had had the opportunity to have their haircut recently. Mother and daughter enjoyed how their hair was handled with tender loving care here. However, it was also a time of fun, as Ada would always entertain Keisha with her stories, while Tanya spent time with Nkechi and Nneka. The twins often had new dance routines that would impress Tanya.

"You two should take part in a dance competition or something."

"Mum doesn't want us to do that. She wants us to study law or medicine."

"But why?"

"She says it's better; that she's not working so hard for us to be dancers. She says that dancing is not a job that will earn us a living."

Tanya was stunned. Both girls were extremely talented, and she thought it was such a shame that their mother could not see that. Again, she wished she knew what she would become when she grew older.

"I don't really mind studying medicine," said Nkechi.

"I don't want to study any of that," said Nneka. "I really want to be like Oti Mabuse."

"I knew you were going to say that. You're always talking about her!" Tanya exclaimed.

"Cos she's simply the best."

"But you know Mum doesn't approve of that," said Nkechi.

"Whatever," replied Nneka. "I know what I want. Anyway, let's put on some music and dance."

Ada's salon was known for her special afro-hair treatments. She used natural products such as cassava, okra, moringa, or aloe vera.

"I heard the most shocking story the other day. A woman dumped her husband, who is a pastor, by the way, after thirty years of marriage."

"What?!?"

"I'm telling you… The worst thing is that a couple of months after they separated, rumour has it she is seeing a man ten years younger."

"Lord have mercy! How could she do that?"

"It's terrible. Apparently, she kicked the pastor out of the house. They have five children, and the youngest is still a minor."

"That's unbelievable. That's not right. I can't believe a Christian woman could do something like that."

"Well, it's happening all over the place. They say women and children have power because they are considered to be vulnerable."

"I just can't believe that it is happening in the church as well. Poor pastor... I pray God gives him the grace..."

They ordered some food. They all ate while the treatments were working their wonders on Tanya's and Keisha's hair. Once the treatments were done, Ada used her magic touch to do amazing hairstyles. It was a low bun, a signature style for Keisha, and plaits for Tanya. Both were happy with the results.

"My friend Janice from the Jubilee Christian Centre told me that a fight broke out between two ladies at church. They were both overweight, and she told me that at some stage, one of them was shouting 'Let me teach her a good lesson!' as she was slapping the other poor lady."

"Ah, ah, ah... Are you for real?" said Keisha, laughing out loud.

"Yep, she got holy slaps, I believe," said Ada, giggling.

Sometimes Keisha could not tell if Ada's stories were genuine or if they were comic church stories that she made up to amuse them.

***

The choir had been permitted to have their first proper rehearsal (with the entire choir present) since lockdown began. They were also going to decide what songs to perform for the MNB competition, though it was not set in stone and may change. Their star song was He Touched Me by Bill Gaither. Jay had modernised the song a little and added some twists to it. They also had to choose a dance routine to accompany the song. Roy, who studied at a prestigious dance school, was chosen to be in charge of the choreography.

It soon became apparent that some choir members disagreed with Jay's arrival. Things did not get off to a good start within the group, since some members felt that they were veterans in the choir. During the singing, it was a battle of the titans between Uche, Mike, Olivia, and Julie. They were fighting among themselves to take the lead, so Zack had to pull them aside and call them to order. He reminded them that Jay was the one to sing the solo part of the songs, not any of them. They were supposed to be the main backing singers. The in fighting was causing quite a stir among the choir members.

***

Zack organised an urgent meeting with Olivia, Julie Jay, Uche, and Mike at his residence. The purpose of the meeting was to try to find a solution allowing the choir to move forward. Then, Zack had a lightbulb moment during the meeting, which he thought would iron things out once and for all. He asked every one of them to write a song and then to come and sing it in front of the judges.

"Whoever wins this little contest will be the one to perform the solo part of the songs in the competition. Not only that, but their song will also be performed in church. You will only have one shot at this."

"Can we not use a song already written?" Olivia asked hopefully.

"No, the purpose here is for you guys to showcase how talented and creative you are."

"That's not fair," protested Mike.

"And why is that?" asked Zack curiously.

"Some of us have never written a song before," Mike responded.

"Well, now is a good time to start," taunted Uche.

"But we have been given very little time to do so," Olivia complained.

"You should already have a song if you're a songwriter by nature."

"It never even crossed my mind to attempt to write a song," Olivia mumbled.

"There you go! It just means that this is not for you, and that's alright, there's nothing wrong with that."

Zack understood them perfectly. He had gone through a rough time as a Christian years ago. He remembered vividly when, as a youngster, he wanted to be a lead singer so badly. He tried out in the auditions at his parent's church. However, he failed miserably. It was a very tough time for him and he felt like a failure. It was as if God had abandoned him, or so he believed. And for a long time, he did not go to church, though his parents tried so hard to encourage him. After all, it was not the end of the world. He did not know that God had something better planned for him. "God will never shut a door without opening another one, a better one," his mother would say philosophically.

"Don't think that I don't understand your predicament. I do. I really, really do—" He sympathised with those who thought that this was an unfair challenge.

"You're not in our shoes," Mike interrupted him, annoyed.

"There's a time that, like you, I really wanted to be a lead singer in the choir. But it was not meant to be. I was not selected. I was disappointed, gutted. Actually, it was one of my darkest hours as a young Christian. I went through a crisis. And for a moment, I lost my faith. See, all my life was about music. I dedicated hours to it. My dream was to be a lead singer."

"What happened?" one of the choir members asked curiously.

"One day, our university choir had a vacancy for a choir leader. A classmate and roommate of mine, Paul, put my name down. He didn't tell me about it and asked me to accompany him somewhere. God used Paul, who was not even Christian, to show me the path that the Lord had for me, and it wasn't what I had in mind for myself. But see how God has turned things around for me. You see, the fact that I was turned down at the auditions was because he had something better for me. He changed the turndown into a turnaround! So, don't despair! Here I am today, standing before you as your choir leader. Who would have thought? He alone knows what we're going to achieve together. And I really have the conviction that He has something great in store for us."

***

Zack had arranged the contest for the following day. He knew it was a big challenge, but at least the winner of this contest would be undeniably established as the choir's lead singer. Olivia and Mike had quit saying that they didn't have the inspiration to write their own song. This left Julie, Jay, and Uche in the race. Zack had summoned the members of the Church Board of Trustees. It was a panel of five people consisting of Steve Pratt and Tom Peckham, respectively solicitor and accountant for the ministry; Assistant Pastor Kweku standing in for Pastor Martin; former choir leader Becky Telford, and Linda Smith, the pastor's PA.

Julie composed a song entitled *You Are My Lord* in English and Twi, a dialect of the Akan tribe. Uche wrote a song entitled *Powerful God* in English and Igbo, a dialect from the Eastern part of Nigeria and *Hold My Hand, Lord, I Can't Do Without You*, was penned by Jay in English. The panel of five judges voted unanimously for Jay. Their feedback was that whilst Julie's and Uche's songs were very touching, they were not competition material and would not have a global reach. Furthermore, Jay's song was a pitch-perfect maestro performance. The song was special and would touch a wider audience.

"Jay's song had a wow factor, or shall I say an X-factor that the other songs did not have," said Becky.

"I totally agree with you," echoed Pastor Kweku.

"It's a very touching song. One that will resonate with many people of all ages, backgrounds, or races," added Linda.

"Though I'm not a Christian, that song really spoke to me," said Tom. "It was sung with deep conviction… There's definitely something about it. It's a very special song."

"If you ask me, the music, the lyrics, the whole song, were all out of this world!" Steve said with much enthusiasm.

"Well, I think we might have had the privilege of discovering our new special talent," Becky concluded, delighted with herself.

Zack was ecstatic that the board agreed with his decision and that Jay had been chosen as the clear winner. At long last, they could put the matter to rest and now focus on the MBN competition. Just as the panel made their announcement, Keisha and Tanya made their entrance. There was an awkward silence. The same question was on everybody's minds. What were the two of them doing at Zack's place?

Finally, Julie was the one who dared to ask the question. "What are you two doing here? Are you staying here?"

Keisha had never felt so embarrassed. Zack didn't know what to say. He had not thought this far ahead. The meeting had lasted longer than scheduled and he had not envisaged the church folks would still be there until early evening.

"Yes, no… *Hhm* …" was all Zack could mumble.

"Guys, it's time for us to excuse ourselves and leave," Pastor Kweku said diplomatically.

The group left as prompted by the Assistant Pastor. Zack and Keisha knew that trouble was brewing, particularly with Julie involved. She detested Keisha and was jealous of her. This feeling had worsened since the arrival of Zack as she thought that he had his eyes on Keisha, something that really annoyed her. She wanted him for herself; she had a plan and Keisha had finally fallen into her trap.

***

"Oh no, I can smell trouble," Zack said.

"Trust Julie to be like that; she is well known for spreading rumours and gossip," Keisha replied.

"We don't have anything to hide," Zack said. "We're not doing anything wrong."

"Never mind. Enough of Julie. Let me go and get dinner ready."

At the dinner table, the trio was enjoying the food Keisha had prepared.

"What's this?"

"It's Filipino style chicken and cabbage. Pearl taught me how to cook this years ago."

"It looks yummy."

"It's delicious and very simple to make."

"Mum, where is Pearl?"

There was a silence. Kesha was taken by surprise.

Zack came to her rescue. "Come on, let's say grace." He had managed to divert Tanya's attention, or so he thought.

"How was work today?"

"I had a very difficult conversation with my boss."

"How is that?"

"A few days ago, he offered me the opportunity to manage one of the IT projects coming up. But I turned him down today."

"It must have been difficult indeed."

"You can say that again. He was extremely disappointed. You see, he had fought for me and put my name forward for the project."

"So, what did you tell him?"

"Oh, just that I had some personal commitments that I could not get out of. But he understood in the end."

***

Tanya was lost in her thoughts while the adults were chatting away. She was worried. What had happened to Pearl? Did she fall sick with COVID-19? Was she in the hospital? Or worse still, had she passed away due to the virus? So many people had died of the deadly virus. Did something happen that forced her to stop being her childminder? Did she leave the United Kingdom and go back to the Philippines for good, Tanya wondered. She mentioned that she had been very homesick lately. She was missing her family and friends because she had not seen them for a while. She was concerned and wondering what had happened to her childminder. Her mother's unwillingness to answer her questions did not help matters.

Chapter IX | Saving Baby Moses

Julie set out to malign Keisha, to get back at her. The very next day, after Jay was confirmed as the lead singer in the choir, she called Pastor Kweku.

"Uncle Kweku, this is a scandal. Keisha is having an affair with Zack."

"Well, we don't know that. Let's not jump to conclusions. There is most likely a perfectly reasonable explanation."

Pastor Kweku was not her biological uncle; she called him this as a sign of respect to an older man. Julie was in her late thirties and was desperate to get married. She had visited multiple times for prayers. She felt that her biological clock was ticking and was becoming very desperate. Her family back home was putting pressure on her to get married. They had asked her to return to Ghana so they could find a suitor for her.

She was fuming to see Keisha in Zack's home and decided to put an end to it. Uncle Kweku told her that Keisha had divorced because she had been wrongly accused of adultery. Her ex-husband left her with Tanya as a newborn baby. He was told by his wife Aunty Fifi, who had found out when Tanya joined the Sunday School years ago. Julie began calling church and choir members to spread the false rumours that Keisha had been having an affair with Zack and that she had previously divorced because she was accused of adultery. The rumours spread like wildfire.

***

At the next rehearsal, both Zack and Keisha felt self-conscious. Some choir members were looking at them suspiciously convinced that they were in a relationship. This was untenable for Zack, who was trying to make his mark as the choir leader. It was another crisis that he could have done without. This was distracting them from their aim, which was preparing for the MBN competition. However, they somehow managed to go through some of the songs they had selected. They were going to sing a selection of these songs during church services in the coming weeks.

Julie couldn't resist stirring up trouble. "Tell us, Keisha, where are you staying at the moment?" she asked slyly and loudly enough so everyone could hear her question. Some people knew about the situation, while others were in the dark, but Julie was about to change that.

"It's none of your business."

"It is our business because we have to make sure that everyone in this choir is in the right standing with the Lord."

"Are you right with the Lord, Julie? You can't be with all the gossip you like to spread about other people."

"Well, I have nothing to hide. And this has nothing to do with me or other people. It's about you and Zack. Are you sleeping together?"

You could hear the brouhaha, and the 'oohs' and 'aahs' in the hall. Keisha was speechless and did not know what to say.

"That's enough now!" interjected Zack. He felt bad for Keisha, as he knew she didn't like being put on the spot. She was an introvert by nature and hated being in such situations.

On the other hand, Julie got what she wanted, which was to publicly corner the two of them. And Keisha didn't outright deny the accusation, so it was making it easier for people to believe her. She thought that if she couldn't have Zack, then she did not mind him being kicked out of the choir. She knew she was being selfish, but she didn't care. This was putting Zack in a shaky situation. As one of the leaders of the church, he was not allowed to have an intimate relationship with any of the choir members without officially informing the elders of his intentions. He could literally lose his position.

"Let's call it a day. Let's meet before church on Sunday for prayers."

"That's if you're still here…" someone whispered maliciously.

***

Zack decided that it was best for Keisha and Tanya to stay at his parents' place in Grove Park to put an end to all the gossip. He spoke to his mum, Cynthia, who was absolutely delighted; she was waiting for them to arrive that evening. Jack, Zack's fraternal twin, was visiting with his Welsh wife, Sara, and their three young boys, Dylan, Evan, and André, named after his Cameroonian maternal great-grandfather. The twin brothers were as different as day and night. Zack, who was the taller and more slender of the two, had very much taken after his parents with their love of gospel music and God; while Jack had no interest in anything remotely to do with the gospel. He was engrossed in his business and was frequently absent due to his work. Even though they had everything they wanted, Sara sometimes felt lonely. They visited his parents on occasions, but often briefly.

The two eldest boys immediately started following Tanya around. She loved kids and always wanted a younger sister or brother. Although she was an only child, she was very giving and caring. After Sara had given them their bath, Tanya offered to read them a Bible story, which they couldn't wait to hear. Toddler André was feeling too sleepy to join them and went straight to bed.

"We are going to hear the story of Moses in the Bible. Have you heard of him?" Tanya had read the story many times and knew it by heart.

The boys shook their heads.

"Once upon a time, there was a very wicked king in a far, far away country called Egypt; they called him Pharaoh. He wanted to kill all the Hebrew boys like you. Why? Because he felt that the people of Israel, another country that is far, far away from us, were much stronger and mightier than the Egyptians."

Tanya would make faces and do some theatrics to amuse the boys. They were enjoying the story and laughing out loud. Occasionally, Jack or Sara would pop in to calm them down or to ask them to be quieter because André was sleeping next door.

"In our story, Moses was just a baby."

"Was he like André?" asked Evan.

"No, he was three months old, so he was smaller. His mother, and sister, Miriam, decided to save him. They put him in a basket and left him among the reeds by the river bank."

"Wow," Dylan exclaimed, really impressed, his eyes wide open. "Like the river we have here in London?"

"Yes, Dylan, that's right. But in our story, it's called the river Nile," replied Tanya.

"But Dad always says the river is dangerous. We're not allowed to get into the river," remarked Evan judiciously.

"Yes, but this was a special time. It was a long, long, long time ago. And guess what?"

The boys were really absorbed in the story and were waiting in anticipation.

"Come on, boys," said Sara as she stuck her head around the door, "time to go to bed."

"Oh no, Mommy," the boys protested, "we want to finish the story."

"We have to wake up early tomorrow to go back home; your daddy has some work to do."

They had heard this too many times. They often had to cut short one outing or another because their father had a successful, busy business that took up all of his time.

"But, Mommy…"

"No buts, come let's go!"

"Bye, lads." Tanya waved them goodbye. She felt sorry for them and understood their frustration.

They wanted to hear the end of the story and were both very disappointed, but they knew better than to argue. They went to bed, dragging their feet.

Tanya thoroughly enjoyed her audience. She had a good rapport with kids and she also really enjoyed storytelling. She went to bed as she was tired; she had been feeling under the weather over the past few days. She dreamt of baby Moses and the ending of the story she had been telling the boys.

She dreamt how Moses's sister watched from a distance to see what would happen next. Pharaoh's daughter went down to the Nile to bathe. She was accompanied by her maids. She saw the basket amongst the reeds and sent one of the maids to get it. She saw Moses crying. She felt sorry for him and recognised him as one of the Hebrew babies.

Moses's sister asked Pharaoh's daughter, "Shall I go and get one of the Hebrew women to nurse the baby for you?"

"Yes, go," she answered.

The girl went and got the baby's mother. Pharaoh's daughter said to her, "Take this baby and nurse him for me, and I will pay you." So, the mother took the baby and nursed him. When the child grew older, she took him to Pharaoh's daughter and he became her son. She called him Moses, which means I drew him out of the water.

In the sitting room, Zack and Jack were catching up. They hadn't really had time to chat since his return from the States.

"So, what's going on between you and Keisha?"

Zack knew better than to deny his feelings for Keisha when he asked. If there was one person he could never hide anything from, it was Jack. Though they were very different in nature, they knew each other inside out.

"I'm drawn to her. There's something special about her. But she's shy; I'm trying to get close to her. I think I'm slowly getting there."

"She seems like a nice woman, attractive as well."

"What about you? How are things with Sara?"

"We're okay, but she's complaining that I'm more concerned about the business than our family. I'm just trying to provide the best for us."

"You need to pay attention to what she's saying, though. She looks a little unhappy."

"Did she say anything to you?"

"No, not really, but I did notice that she wasn't her usual self. Be careful, bro. You do need to slow down a bit."

"I can't; not now. I still need a couple of years to establish the company and then I will be able to take it easy."

"Don't jeopardise your family for your business success. Don't leave it too late."

"I hear you, bro. You also need to settle down, you know."

"I would like to… Keisha would be the ideal woman for me. It's not just the attraction I have towards her, but also, I have a sense of peace when I'm around her."

"By the way, I saw Eileen the other day. We spoke for a while. She was in a bad way after you split with her."

"I feel bad thinking about that… I know I should have handled it better, but I was young and stupid, I guess. She accused me of dumping her after helping me go through college. But the truth of the matter is that she wasn't interested in God. I could see we were incompatible and couldn't go through with the wedding thing."

"Well, she went through a bad patch with alcohol addiction. But she's in a better place now; she's married with a kid."

"I'm glad to hear that. I felt 'cursed' and thought that's why I couldn't find the right woman after that. I hope she's forgiven me."

"I think she's well over you, don't you worry."

"That's awesome! I'm relieved."

***

Keisha had managed to contact Jasmine, one of Pearl's friends. They had organised a candlelight vigil for Perla as she was known within the Filipino community. They were also collecting money to repatriate the body back to the Philippines where her family lived. She decided to attend the ceremony and gave a donation.

"I'm so sorry about the sudden passing of Pearl," Keisha said to Jasmine sadly.

"It's so frustrating that the media has not covered this at all. We feel like she is invisible," she said with her very distinct Filipino accent.

"They might have their reasons."

"Maybe, but the family feels that they have not been kept informed."

"Do you have a contact for any of the family who can speak English? I want to speak with them so that I can personally give my condolences. Pearl was such a big part of our lives."

"Yes, sure. I will WhatsApp you the details."

"That's perfect. Thank you, Jasmine."

"That's alright. I'm happy to be able to help. It's so sad though. She was in the prime of her life. Her life came to an abrupt end; just like that."

"I know it's very hard to take. I will keep you posted and let you know if I hear anything."

"Thank you so much, Keisha. Perla really loved you and Tanya. She thought so highly of you. You were almost like family to her."

"I feel the same. It's such a loss, you know. We have known each other for over five years. I have such fond memories of her. The least we can do is to track down the killers. We won't give up, that's a promise."

"Thank you so much, Keisha. Bye."

"Bye, Jasmine, and all the best."

Keisha then made contact via WhatsApp with one of Pearl's cousins, Benjie. He was a nurse in the States and had come to the Philippines for a vacation when he learnt the sad news of his relative's passing.

"It was such a shock to us. How did this happen? And why do we not have any details?"

"First of all, I would like to say that we are so sorry about Pearl's death. My daughter could not make it today, unfortunately."

"Thank you. All we know is that she died suddenly. Nobody was willing or could even tell us what happened. We're totally in the dark here."

Benjie appeared to be very upset.

"I'm so sorry, I thought the police were keeping you posted with the latest developments in the case. I cannot say much due to the ongoing investigation. However, I wanted to share that we are saddened by her death. Pearl was such a lovely lady. We had such good memories of our time with her. My daughter and I will miss her so dearly."

"How did you come to know Perla?"

"She was my childminder and much more. She was part of the family. We would go on short vacations together sometimes. She was such a fun lady. She dreamed of becoming an actress. It's sad to see that her life was cut short in such a dramatic way."

"She was my little cousin. She was indeed fun-loving, always taking part in one school play or the other; always the life of the party. Very quickly, she learnt to speak English because she wanted to leave the Philippines. She dreamt of fame and stardom. She sacrificed so much. Even leaving her ex-boyfriend behind because she wanted to forge ahead. She initially wanted to go to the States, but when it didn't happen, she managed to settle in the United Kingdom. She enjoyed being in London. She visited many European countries and would always WhatsApp photos or post them on her Facebook page. She really hoped that things would work out. It's a real pity that things ended up like this."

"Yes, it's so sad. So very sad." Keisha could tell that it was helping him to talk to her, even though she was a stranger to him.

"It's comforting to see that my cousin had people like you around her, who genuinely loved her. We, in the family, also really appreciate that you've made an effort to reach out."

Now she was the one to feel very emotional. They were both fighting back the tears. Keisha was clenching her fists. The guilt was also there, so overwhelming. But she needed to make some kind of gesture for Pearl's sake. She felt that it was important to communicate with a family member though it was difficult for her to come face-to-face with a relative's grief. It was difficult but necessary.

"She hadn't returned home in a while. I hadn't seen her for years. But from time to time, we would communicate via WhatsApp. She was even thinking of visiting, as we have family members scattered throughout the States. But again, that didn't happen."

Keisha did not mention that a recent heartbreak had actually brought some doubts about her future in the United Kingdom. Thinking about Pearl's wanting to move made her wonder if perhaps it was time for her to relocate for good, but she was unsure of where to go.

"I know that she had been feeling homesick. She was hoping to travel, but obviously, the pandemic and the lockdown made things a little complicated."

"When do you think we will have more details?"

"I'm not sure, Benjie, but as soon as there are any developments, I will let you know."

"I will give you my contact details in the States, just in case. I'm in Manilla for another month and then I will return to California."

"Okay, no worries. Once again, our sincere condolences to the family."

"Thanks, Keisha. I will pass it on. Thank you for taking the time to talk to me."

Keisha decided it was also time for her to do something she had not done for years. She took the step to go to the cemetery and visit her son's grave. She had not been there in years. The grief was just too much to bear. A mother should never have to bury her child, she mused. She felt different this time around; she expected to break down and weep. The overwhelming pain she usually felt when she came to the graveyard had vanished. She had not killed her son intentionally; it was an unfortunate accident. She had come a long way; she recognised that her faith had played a big part in her recovery and inner healing. She had this sense of peace that she would see him again one day. But here on earth, this chapter of her life had long come to an end.

"So long, Charlie," she whispered. She had found closure at long last.

Chapter X | 'Cast the First Stone!'

Pastor Kweku was preaching a strong message this Sunday morning. One could hear a pin drop. "The title of my message is 'Anyone of you who is without sin, cast the first stone!' taken from the gospel of John, chapter 8. It is so easy to judge other people. Yet no one is perfect! Remember, we were all sinners in need of a Saviour. We were fornicating, lying, and stealing, but the Lord rescued us. Remember where we've come from. We were ignorant, in darkness. The Lord cleansed us. He washed away all of our sins. So, what makes you think that you're in a position to judge or condemn? Judge not that you be not judged. 'Remove the plank from your own eye, and then you will see clearly to remove the speck from your brother's eye.' it says in Matthew 7."

Some members of the choir were uneasy. All eyes were on Julie, Keisha, and Zack.

"We all know the story of Joseph and Potiphar's wife. Turn with me to the book of Genesis, chapter 39," he continued. "The Bible did not bother to give us her name, as if to show how immaterial she was. She gave herself to Joseph on a platter of gold. But he denied her the privilege because he had both the faith and the fear of God. He ran away from the scene. And in her anger, she accused him of rape. She had only one piece of circumstantial evidence against Joseph: his garment. She kept his garment as proof of his so-called attempted rape. Brethren, it seemed from the outside that her little story was true. But it was all a pack of lies! She had concocted the tale to get back at Joseph in disappointment, frustration, and anger. Let's be careful not to judge too quickly when we don't have all the facts. Potiphar was deceived by his uncontrollable, wayward wife. He believed her and lost his top worker in the process."

Julie's rumour had gone round the church. She was seething as she was under the impression that Pastor Kweku's sermon was targeting her. How could her fellow countryman do this to her, she thought. After all that she shared with him on the phone the other day, she thought that she had won him over. It was obviously not the case. Pastor Kweku understood that the stakes were too high for the ministry. They could not afford to lose Zack and not make it to the MNB competition. Abundant Life Ministries was banking on the competition to promote the ministry.

"Let's not forget something. I said that she was immaterial. However, she played a vital role in this story: The Lord used her to catapult Joseph to his destiny, to the next chapter of his life. He ended up in prison. What seemed like an unfortunate event would turn out to be a blessing in disguise.

For in prison, he met his helper of destiny, his divine connection. His hour of triumph came when, through the king's butler, Joseph was released from jail and was promoted to be second in command after Pharaoh. So always remember that when you go through a tragedy as Joseph did, there is a light at the end of the tunnel. A turnaround, a breakthrough, might be at your doorstep." The members of the church expressed their approbation. Some were standing and clapping, others were shouting 'Amen', and 'Alleluia!'

"We had a great example of this in church with Ben or Pastor Ben as we all know him. He almost lost his life recently. But he saw the bigger picture. He saw the souls of these young people. It was a selfless act at such a young age and he refused to press charges. What maturity. We should all learn from this young man. We should thank God for him."

The whole church clapped in appreciation for Ben's attitude. The atmosphere instantly lightened. Ben and his family were not in church that day. But Pastor Kweku had made a point of phoning the young man to express his appreciation and that of the entire church.

The choir then performed some of the songs that they had selected for the competition. The performance included choreography that was prepared by Roy. Kim Knightley was doing some ballet dancing during one of the songs. Suddenly, her wig went flying across the stage. It was surreal. Everyone in the audience who had their eyes open was able to see the whole scene and her very short hair. They could not believe their eyes and started laughing. Kim ran off the stage into the back room, mortified. This lightened the atmosphere, which had been tense and sombre after Pastor Kweku's sermon, though this had been achieved at Kim's expense.

After the service, Zack and Keisha were summoned to Pastor Kweku's office. "I'm concerned that the wrong impression is being given," he said very diplomatically.

"It's not what people think, Pastor. We're not going out together," Zack replied.

"Well, what's going on then?"

"Keisha and Tanya were staying at my place for a couple of nights as she was sorting out some personal issues. It was an emergency, but she's now staying at my parents' house for a while, till things get back to normal."

"I hope all is well?" Pastor Kweku asked inquisitively.

"Nothing to worry about," answered Keisha. "We just need to take a break for a while and we're staying at Zack's parents. Nothing untoward has happened, I promise."

"I'm glad to hear that," he said. "I will let the Board of Trustees know of the situation. I will recommend that no further action is to be taken."

"Thanks, Pastor," they said in unison.

***

Zack went to his Muay Thai kickboxing training to let off some steam. He started practising martial arts, and, in particular, judo, as a youngster. He had discovered Muay Thai kickboxing when he moved to the States. This was martial arts at its highest level. He would train whenever he had the time and had met a bunch of guys at the club. They would connect either in the evenings after work or at weekends. They would first do some workouts and practice some Muay Thai boxing techniques, then sometimes finish up with a three-round fight. It could be gruesome, but it kept him fit. Some were training to compete at national or even world-class levels. To Zack, it was just a hobby.

"So, are you ready to take the world by storm, Hitoshi?" Zack would tease him.

"The sky's the limit for me. I qualified for a tournament in Thailand next year."

"Good for you."

"I'm trying to organise some sparring with other Muay Thai fighters."

"What, you think we're not good enough?" He laughed with self-derision.

"Not that; it's just standard practice. The more you practise, the more you improve and develop new techniques. Same as any other sports."

"Well, I'll be cheering you on."

"Are you not interested in competing at a professional level?"

"Not at all."

"You're pretty good and have some pretty impressive techniques."

"Ah no, it's just to keep me fit. I have no intention of pursuing it as a career," Zack said dismissively.

"Alright, I can see there's no changing your mind."

"Yes, my mind is made up on that."

"It's a pity. I wish I had your physique and your techniques."

Hitoshi was of average height, with a slim but extremely strong build. On the other hand, Zack was 6' 1" and slightly muscular.

***

Keisha and Tanya headed off to Sharon and Caroline Spencer's for their monthly meeting. They were going to stay overnight. Sharon, Caroline, and her husband Peter had been in Abundant Life years before Keisha and Tanya. Peter, who was also a member of the choir, usually left the house while the ladies' get-together was happening. They arrived earlier, as Keisha wanted to talk to Sharon.

"You look exhausted. What's up with you, Keisha?"

"It's been rough the last month or so. I've had to deal with a lot at work, in church, and my personal life, and it's tough."

"Have you prayed about it?" Sharon asked.

"Yes, I have." She hesitated.

"Is there anything you want me to know?"

Sharon was a good judge of character and a woman full of wisdom. She would always encourage Keisha to pray.

"Well, you know Zack, right?"

"Who is he?"

"The new choir leader."

"Oh yeah, silly me. I heard all the rumours. Peter told me a bit, about what's going on. Although, you know he didn't expand on it… Zack is doing great, isn't he?"

"Yes, things are going fine."

"So why do you have that look on your face?"

"Well, I'm not sure what is going on between us. I've had to take a break, and I'm staying with his parents at the moment."

"Why?"

"Oh, it's a long story, but it's temporary." Keisha didn't want to elaborate.

"Are you attracted to him?"

"I'm not sure, it's been such a long time…"

"You've got to let go of your past, Keisha."

"'Don't dwell on the past,' Isaiah 43:18. I know that verse all too well, Sharon. It was one of several scriptures that I memorised years ago when I went through that situation with my ex-husband and Charlie."

"You have to move on and overcome your fears."

"But you know how I suffered over the loss of Charlie and the divorce with Felix."

"Do you want to be alone for the rest of your life? You have to give love another chance."

"I don't know."

"Well, you have to take the risk, you know. Give it a try."

"He hasn't said anything, and you know how old-fashioned I am."

"I'm not telling you to chase him. But you have to make an effort to be friendlier, less uptight; you know what I mean? Or else one of those lovely ladies in the church will be too glad to grab him all to themselves."

"I know! Julie for instance."

"Really? I don't think she stands a chance."

"Why do you say that? How do you know?"

"She strikes me as being too forward and men don't usually like that. Anyway, what I'm trying to say is that competition is usually stiff among the ladies in churches in general, as there are fewer men."

"I just wonder why he's not married yet. He seems like a good man, so why is he still single?"

"You're too suspicious. He might simply not have found the right woman, that's all. Don't go reading into things too much."

The rest of the group progressively joined them. The Bible study was led by Maëva while Keisha handled the prayer part. This was the opportunity for her to ask for prayers from her Christian sisters without going into details. They prayed for her personally, her situation at work, and in church. She had a sense of peace that everything was going to be alright. Things were not as bad as they had seemed, after all. Keisha felt much better and really relied upon the prayer support of these dear sisters.

After the prayers, Sharon treated them to some Canadian specialities. It was a delectable meal, off the beaten track of spicy food. The ladies thoroughly enjoyed the various dishes and they all felt that it was a nice change.

They had decided to watch a movie this time around. They opted for the 2009 movie Blind Side starring Sandra Bullock, for which she won the coveted award for Best Actress. It depicted the story of seventeen-year-old African American Michael (Big Mike) adopted by a Caucasian family, the Tuohys. His athleticism and physical stature earned him admission into a Christian school, despite his poor academic credentials. Finding himself homeless, he was walking along the road one cold winter evening, inappropriately dressed for the season, when Leigh Anne Tuohy (Sandra Bullock), whose children went to the same school, spotted him. She invited him to stay at their home for the night. Eventually, Big Mike would end up staying for much longer than that. It turned out that, after learning how to play American football, he was a talented offensive lineman (with some push from Leigh Anne). He also managed to improve his grades through the private tuition paid by his adoptive family. This allowed him to play at the university level. Several prestigious schools competed to recruit him.

He eventually settled for the University of Mississippi, otherwise known as 'Ole Miss'. However, this proved controversial, with the Tuohys accused of unduly influencing him to make this choice, as the family had close links with the university. Big Mike ends up confronting Leigh Anne about her motives. He did eventually stick with his original decision of attending 'Ole Miss'.

There was a debate at the end of the movie with Ada and Thandi questioning whether they would have adopted him so quickly if he had been a problematic, challenging, badly behaved teenager. Would they have loved him even though he had come with issues? They felt that the Tuohys had somehow benefitted from his successful career as a football star. The rest of the group, Keisha included, felt that their adoption of a child of a different race, and providing the necessary support for the youngster to achieve his grades and to learn how to play American football, was honourable of them. There was nothing wrong with it. After all, how many black people would do or would have done this? Moreover, who would not want to adopt a trouble-free child? She remembered numerous times in Atlanta when a family would allow social services to put up a relative's child for adoption or put them in a foster home because the parents were either too poor, incarcerated, on crack, heroin, or had a cocaine addiction.

Tanya was sleeping in the same room as Caroline. She was in a deep sleep, dreaming of Josiah. He was the descendant of King David and King Solomon. His father Amon, King of Judah, had died. His servants had plotted against him and had killed him in his own house. Josiah became king when he was eight years old, which in itself was an achievement. He did what was right and followed in the footsteps of his ancestor David.

As a teenager, he began to pray and seek God. He spent hours praying and was loyal to God. When he was twenty, he decided to rid Judah and Jerusalem of false religion and idol worship. He removed all the evil altars and paraphernalia that were used by the fake priests. He also did away with the evil priests who had indulged in idolatry. He did so in the cities of Manasseh, Ephraim, and Simeon.

Tanya was very agitated when all this was going on in the dream. She ended up waking Caroline.

"Hey, Tanya. Are you alright?"

"Mhm," Tanya answered, a little panicked and very disorientated.

"You had a nightmare."

"I was dreaming of the story we heard at Bible study tonight."

"Which one?"

"The story of King Josiah and how faithful and loyal he was to God."

"Ah, okay that one. Yeah, he was a pretty impressive king for a boy of that age. But why were you so fidgety in your dream? He was a good king."

"Yes, but I dreamt that he went and asked his men to destroy all the false altars and how he killed the fake priests. These were scenes of violence, pretty scary."

"Okay I see," she said. "Let's go back to sleep. Night, night, Tanya."

"Night, night, Caroline."

Chapter XI | Young Solomon's Request for Wisdom

Finsbury Park Metropolitan Police station was a modern building that was built in the late 2000s. Finsbury Park itself was a multicultural neighbourhood of Harringay in North London with a strong sense of community. Thefts and violence against a person were the most common crimes carried out. Hence, the police station was busy. The police had recently resumed conducting face-to-face interviews.

"You have some explaining to do, Mrs Campbell," Inspector Detective Hunt stated matter-of-factly.

"What do you mean?" retorted Keisha.

"We have made enquiries, questioned the neighbours. Nobody heard or saw anything. As far as we know, the last person who saw the victim alive is you, Mrs Campbell."

"I don't understand, what—"

"I get the impression that you have not told us the full story," he interrupted.

Keisha felt uneasy with his line of questioning. Her heart was pounding and she started to feel as if she could not breathe properly. She had to hold herself together; otherwise her attitude might incriminate her.

All of this reminded her of Charlie's tragic death. The police had come to investigate the circumstances surrounding the unfortunate event. They were not sympathetic and had implied that she had been negligent as a mother. They had investigated her life inside out, even making sure she had not taken out an insurance policy in the States to cash in upon his death. It was a nightmare; one that made her wary of the police. This also explained why she was so nervous around them. Eventually, it was ruled an accident, as a neighbour came forward as a witness to corroborate her account. But the grief she had experienced and the subsequent allegations from the police had left her devastated. It took her a long time to recover and she had to go through therapy to overcome her anxiety and trauma.

"The preliminary results of the autopsy revealed that she [Pearl[died by asphyxiation, which confirms what you stated. However, there are some elements of this crime that we cannot piece together. There was no attempted rape, kidnapping, or theft, though we would need you to confirm that nothing has been taken. Do you have any valuables in the house such as money, jewellery, paintings, artefacts, etc. that the killer may have been after?"

"No, I don't actually, except some jewellery."

"Who knew that your childminder was going to be at your house?"

"I didn't tell anybody; it was a last-minute thing. I don't know if Pearl told anyone."

"We contacted her next of kin, but nothing came out of it. It's a mystery, and we have no leads at present. The question remains as to why she was killed at your place. From our investigations, she wasn't linked to any drug gangs and she had no criminal record. So far, we have no motive. Do you have any ideas?"

The last thing she wanted was to be accused of obstructing the course of justice. At the same time, she didn't want the killers to realise that she had escaped. She had to think fast.

"No, I don't. Am I a suspect in this investigation, Detective?"

"Well, no, not yet anyway. I just have several scenarios that I want to run by you to see what you think, Mrs Campbell. Scenario number one, the killer was caught while trying to commit a crime of some sort and killed your childminder to get rid of her as a witness. But the question is why go to the extreme length of killing her? He could have just knocked her unconscious and escaped, unless, of course, they knew each other and he had no choice but to eliminate her. But the location of the crime is what really makes this unlikely.

"The second scenario is that you killed her for some unknown reason. Although, from our investigation, you seem to have had a good relationship with her. You've known each other for years. You trusted her enough to leave your daughter with her. Your neighbours have mentioned that they've never heard or seen any incidents, arguments, or fighting between you. If anything, quite the contrary. Pearl was considered almost like a member of your family.

"The other scenario would be that it is a case of mistaken identity. The murderer thought he killed you instead of your childminder. As you said, the place was dark. Also, the childminder was not meant to have stayed that night according to you. I think that the first scenario is unlikely. Why? Because the childminder's presence at your residence was not planned. Also, why would they come to her place of work late at night to get rid of her? That's too risky. The second scenario is a little bit more plausible than the first. This could be a crime of passion. You may have been in a relationship with her as neighbours noted that you were quite close. Maybe you were lovers and something went wrong, who knows?"

"What?!? I'm not a lesbian! I was married before, you know."

"And, so what? You could be bisexual. After your divorce, you may have decided to come out of the closet and be openly lesbian; anything is possible these days. The only loophole in this scenario is that the whole thing doesn't match your profile. It fits more with the behaviour of a cold-blooded killer rather than an overly protective mother whose child is only a few feet away from the scene of the altercation. You're known to be protective towards your daughter, so it's highly unlikely that you would run the risk of exposing her to such an act of violence. Also, you would have needed an enormous amount of strength to choke Pearl without her having the time to scream and alert your daughter that something was going down that night. So, we can safely rule this out as well. I want to focus on the last scenario. I have reasons to believe that this is an unfortunate case of mistaken identity. Do you have any enemies that may want to kill you?"

Keisha remained quiet for a while. She was in a dilemma. If she opened up, she would have to give the killer's motive and she was not prepared for that yet. She couldn't lie either because of her principles, and this would only make the situation worse. She decided to remain silent to avoid incriminating herself in any way.

"Mrs Campbell, may I remind you that it is absolutely imperative that you cooperate with our investigation. Lying, giving false information, or false details is tantamount to perverting the course of justice and is an offence." Keisha was just looking at Detective Hunt, not moving an inch. He realised that he wasn't going to get anything out of her, so decided to go and talk to his superior.

Tanya was waiting in the corridor for her mother to come out of the detective's office. While waiting, she fell asleep. She could see in her dream how teenage Solomon inherited his father's kingdom. One day, the Lord appeared to Solomon in a dream at night. God said, "Ask! What shall I give you?"

Solomon answered, "Now, Lord my God, you made me a servant king in place of my father David. But I am only a little child and do not know how to carry out my duties among great people too numerous to count or number. So, give your servant a discerning heart to govern your people and to distinguish between right and wrong."

God was pleased that Solomon had asked for this. He said, "Since you have asked for this and not for long life or wealth for yourself, nor have asked for the death of your enemies but for discernment in administering justice, I will do what you have asked. I will give you a wise and discerning heart so that there will never have been anyone like you, nor will there ever be. Moreover, I will give you what you have not asked for – both wealth and honour – so that in your lifetime you will have no equals among kings. And if you walk in obedience to me and keep my decrees and commands as David, your father did, I will give you a long life."

Then Solomon awoke and realised he had been dreaming. Tanya's own dream continued.

One day, two prostitutes came to the king. They had both given birth to a son.

"During the night, this woman's son had died because she lay on him. So, she woke up in the middle of the night and took my son from my side while I slept and laid her dead son on my lap. When I woke up, there he was, dead. But when I looked at him closely in the morning, I saw that it wasn't the son I had given birth to."

"No! The living one is my son, the dead one is yours."

The two women continued arguing before the king.

"Bring me a sword," said King Solomon. So, they brought a sword. Then the king gave an order, "Cut the living child into two and give half to one and a half to the other."

The woman whose son was still alive was deeply touched and out of love for her son, said to the king, "Please, my Lord, give her the living baby! Don't kill him!"

"Neither I nor you shall have him. Cut him in two!" said the other prostitute.

Then the king gave a ruling. "Give the living baby to the first woman. Do not kill him, she is his mother."

When the whole country heard the verdict, everybody was in awe of the king because he had shown great wisdom in granting justice.

***

Detective Inspector Hunt was talking to the Detective Chief Inspector. "Has she spoken?"

"Nope, Chief. She's not said a word. But I have a sense that she is hiding something. The thing is that we don't have enough to take her into custody. Her record is spotless. There's just something in her story that doesn't add up though."

"Release her and put her under surveillance. She might unwittingly lead us to the killers. I will get two of our guys to monitor her, although we're already quite stretched, with social distancing and self-isolation going on at the moment. Let's try to keep her a little while until we put these arrangements in place. Ask her to write a second statement. Also, we need to go and dig a little more into her past. Talk to her family, boyfriend/girlfriend, close friends, colleagues, etc."

"I understand that she is an African American who has been living in the United Kingdom for a number of years."

"Get as much information about her life as possible. We need a complete profile of the type of person that she is. We need to know if she is capable of committing such a horrible crime. Now, do you think she did it?"

"I don't think so, but she might know or at least suspect who did."

"So, you will need to find out who and why. And also, why is she not forthcoming with the information? Who is she protecting? We need a motive for this to stick."

"Yes, boss, I'll get to work straight away and keep you posted."

***

They managed to keep Keisha and Tanya delayed until two detectives were available to keep track of them. Detectives Penny Kelleher and Andy Slim were assigned to the case. They followed the mother and daughter as soon as they left the police station. They then waited in the car outside Zack's parents' house.

"That's not her address."

"Do you know who lives on the property?" Detective Kelleher asked.

"I haven't got a clue."

"I suppose her house is not yet accessible due to the investigation, so she's probably staying with some friends."

"Right, let's find a nosy and talkative neighbour who will give us some clues as to who they are."

"Where do we start?"

"I will walk around and see if there is anyone I can strike up a casual conversation with."

"You certainly have the skills to succeed." Detective Kelleher laughed. They had worked together on a number of cases and made a great team. Detective Slim was more of a people's person; he knew how to build rapport with anyone. He would work his magic and people would invariably open up. He had the knack of being able to befriend the unsuspecting witness or suspect. Without fail, they would give out invaluable information to him.

Detective Kelleher's strengths lay elsewhere. She would do the research and was good at profiling and steering the investigation in the right direction. She would rarely come up with a dead lead. She obtained the address and postcode of the house through their system. She then went online to find out that the owners of the property were Clive and Cynthia Armstrong. Pensioners, parents, and grandparents. He was a retired doctor and she was a retired nurse. So, what was their relationship with Keisha? They would probably not find the answer online. A breakthrough was more likely to happen by talking to Keisha's entourage.

***

Pastor Ben was in Pastor Kweku's office. He had just had a meeting with Adam and Oliver, the two culprits who had pushed him into the lake. They were starting their classes that evening.

"I would like to know, what got into you that day? Why did you have to push me? What did I do to you?"

"It's not you, man. I've nothing against you. We were just high. We'd been smoking weed. We weren't in our right senses," Adam replied.

"Anyway, I've forgiven you."

"I really appreciate that, man," Oliver said.

"We owe you one, man. Sorry, I really didn't mean to…" He sounded really apologetic. Ben could see that he meant it.

"And us escaping the 'juve' is dope, man."

"What's the juve?"

"Juvenile institution, we call it 'juve'."

"Yeah, a couple of our friends have ended up there, you see what I'm saying. They're in there for theft, possession of drugs, knife crime, and the likes."

"Okay, guys, I will be the one in charge of your discipleship classes," said Pastor Kweku, interrupting their conversation. "It's going to be once a week, for an hour. Now, do you have Bibles?" The youngsters shook their heads. "No, we don't."

"I have some here for you. Next time you have to come with notebooks. You probably know that I have to report back to Ben's parents. And if you do not abide by the rules, Ben's promise not to press charges will be rescinded. Is this understood?"

"Yes," they replied in unison.

"I do hope that something good will come out of this. I would really like to see you change and off the streets after all this," Ben said to the two youngsters. He sounded so much more mature than them. "Ben, you can stay in the class or you're free to go." Ben left Pastor Kweku's office. He then met Tanya, who was waiting for her mum's choir to end.

"You alright, Tanya?"

"Yes, and you?"

"I am, actually. I just saw Adam and Oliver."

"Who are they?"

"The guys who pushed me into the lake."

"Oh," she said.

"I had a little chat with them."

"What did they say?"

"From what they said, I could tell they were sorry. They were no longer playing tough."

"You remind me of young Solomon. You have so much wisdom, Pastor Ben. You're a star for not pressing charges against them."

"I used the opportunity to have the gospel taught to them. What good would prison do for them? My teacher said that jail turns young offenders into hardened criminals. I didn't want that for them. I'm sure Pastor Kweku will help them."

"That's good."

"You know Pastor Kweku will drum the gospel into their heads. They won't know what's hit them." They laughed. They were great friends and had developed a good bond throughout the years. She saw him as a big brother and always sought his advice.

"And how are you feeling now?" She had been worried about him.

"Great actually. Mum's been cooking my favourite dishes and baking cakes for me. And I haven't had to attend my classes. But Dad said I'll go back next week because I seem to have recovered."

"Are you happy about that?"

"It's alright. I miss some of my classmates. And I probably have a lot of catching up to do."

"Right, I have to go now. Mum is waiting for me; bye."

"See you later, Tanya."

Chapter XII | Hotel Arrival

Canary Wharf MBN studios were a state-of-the-art centre of excellence for music and dance. It was a four-storey building. Twenty choirs had been chosen to take part in the competition. They had come from all over the United Kingdom, as far as Northern Ireland. To take part in the competition, entrants needed to be an amateur choir, singing gospel for an organisation or church.

For the auditions, the choirs had to perform one hymn and a more contemporary gospel song. The hymn that Zack eventually selected, and was approved by the church, was the timeless British hymn *My Hope is Built on Nothing Less*. The second one was *O' Happy Day*. The choirs were free to make whatever musical arrangements they wished, including *acapella*. The Abundant Life choir felt intimidated by the crowds, the other choirs, the surroundings, and the panel. But they were also full of excitement and trepidation.

For the competition, they had all booked three nights in the same hotel, which was a short walk from the MBN studio. It was a four-star hotel, with a restaurant, bar, gym, and parking. The competition would start on Friday and would close on Sunday. They arrived at 6.30p.m. on Thursday to register for the competition. Zack had asked everybody to meet fifteen minutes before to make sure that they were all in the hotel lobby on time. This would also give them time for prayer, to rehearse the following morning, and perform in the afternoon.

"Are we all here?" asked Zack. He went down the list to ensure that everyone had made it on time. Just then, Keisha, Tanya, and his parents made it to the lobby. Keisha realised how much she had missed him, which took her by surprise. Her heart started pounding, and she was somehow flushed and awkward. What was happening to her? Could it be...? No, she said to herself. They had not seen each other for a while, even though she was still staying at his parents' house. She had grown very close to them. Tanya even treated them as her grandparents. Keisha felt less burdened as a single mum with their help. She felt serene with Cynthia and Clive. Both parents had noticed the chemistry between Zack and Keisha, but kept it to themselves. The group, including Julie, could also see it.

"Hi, guys, are you alright?" asked Zack. "Mum, Dad, and Tanya, you can go ahead to the reception and check-in. We can meet up later for dinner."

"Alright, Son. Let us know when you guys are done," his dad said.

They waved goodbye and went towards the reception. Keisha did not say a word as she was conscious that the rest of the group were following what was going on very closely.

"You're all welcome," said the front office manager, Agnieszka Piotrowski. She spoke with a slight Polish accent, but was very articulate. She was also hard-working and highly efficient, which is why senior management entrusted her with taking charge of the various groups that had come for the competition. She was flanked by her Brazilian Personal Assistant, Linda Da Costa, who was a touch warmer and friendlier than her boss. It was a good team overall.

"I'm Agnieszka," she added, "and Linda is my Personal Assistant. We will be taking care of you for the duration of your stay here. Any issues let Linda or myself know. It's usually quicker to go to Linda, as I might be elsewhere on the top floor. Please ensure that you register yourselves with Linda. Once registration is completed, you will be given a badge. This will be evidence that you are part of the competition and will give you access to all the amenities, such as the gym, the bar, so on and so forth. You will also have to sign an agreement. Please read the instructions and the terms and conditions for the competition carefully. For instance, you're not allowed to use your camera. Any photos taken are the property of the organisers, as they have the exclusive right to post any content. Following your registration, please proceed to the reception."

"Are we allowed to post photos, video clips, and the likes on social media?" asked a member of one of the other choirs.

"No, that's the reason for the agreement. You will see it when you get to the reception. The rules are pretty strict. Shreya Gupta, the senior receptionist, will look after you. She will be the best person to answer any questions regarding the agreement. You can then go to your rooms after registration. Tomorrow is your first round, so you're free tonight. Enjoy your stay and may the best choir win," she said, sounding slightly nervous. "Now, over to you Linda."

"Hey, I'm Linda. I will try to help you get through this evening as smoothly as possible. Hopefully, it will not be too unpleasant for you. I know having to queue and wait around till all the formalities are completed can be a bit too much for some. As Agnieszka said earlier on, the first round will be tomorrow, starting at 2p.m."

All choir members were listening attentively.

"Please follow me," said Linda with a broad smile.

"Linda, do you know if the panel has arrived yet?" asked Zack.

"I have no idea," she said with her friendly smile. "But I could find out for you," she volunteered. "Why, is there anything the matter?"

"No, not really. I just want to find out who the judges are, that's all."

"I'll ask Agnieszka, she will know. She is in charge of taking care of the event organisers, including the panel."

At the reception area, Shreya Gupta and her team of junior receptionists were inundated with new arrivals early in the evening.

"We have the agreement that Agnieszka or Linda must have mentioned to you. Please sign and date it, and return it to us with the registration form. This agreement states that you have to respect the privacy, confidentiality, and exclusivity clauses. Any breach can lead to expulsion from the competition and may even lead to reimbursement of all expenses incurred by the organisers, including the hotel bill, food, etc. You may also have to pay a fine or damages for a breach of the terms and conditions as this may cause the organisers financial losses due to information and so on being leaked. Please read this agreement carefully before you sign it so that you are aware of your liabilities."

The competition participants were concerned about the agreement and were looking at each other. Was this not too heavy-handed? Sharing the moment with family and friends was part of the excitement. Anyway, they had been warned. They would just have to comply with the rules.

Meanwhile, Shreya had issues of her own. She had received some bad news from home. Her mother, who lived in New Delhi, was suffering from cardiovascular disease. She urgently needed coronary artery bypass grafting. It was a costly heart surgery. She needed to raise thousands of pounds for the surgery to go ahead. She had thought of doing some fundraising. However, there was not much time, as the operation had to go ahead as soon as possible. Shreya felt for her mum with whom she was very close. Her heart was heavy; she felt like she was carrying a huge burden on her shoulders. But she had to find a way to save her mum, who had sacrificed so much to send her to school in the United Kingdom. There has got to be a solution to this, she thought to herself.

***

Zack's group had spent four months preparing themselves for the competition. There had been in-fighting, fallouts, and reconciliations. The choir had reached a watershed moment and had made it this far. This was their opportunity to showcase their talents. Zack felt that he had managed to leave his imprint on the group, although the road to the competition had been a bumpy ride. How well they would fare compared to the other choirs, he was not sure. However, having worked as an assistant choir leader in America, he strongly believed that their vocals and music arrangements would stand out – he hoped they would anyway. They had worked so hard to fine-tune the music. He prayed that they had done enough over the last few months to impress the panel.

He also couldn't keep Keisha out of his mind. He was determined to make his feelings and intentions known to her. Enough of this cat and mouse game. After all, they were two adults. He wanted something serious; he was tired of superficial relationships that led nowhere. He joined Keisha so that they could meet up with his parents and Tanya to go out for dinner.

"How's it going, Keisha? How are you and Tanya getting on with my parents?"

"Your parents are so lovely. Your mum taught me how to cook some good African and Jamaican dishes."

"I bet she did! She loves cooking. What's your favourite?"

"They're all yummy. It's hard to pick just one. I enjoy the fresh grilled Croaker – Douala style she calls it – with special spices found in Cameroon. I can't remember the names but I wrote them down somewhere."

Zack smiled. He knew what his mum was up to, but kept it to himself. He did not want Keisha to withdraw from him.

***

As Zack went to the reception to call his parents, Keisha thought it strange that it was the second time that she had experienced a connection with Cameroon. Her ex-husband originally came from there. And Zack was half-Cameroonian. Destiny had a way of playing tricks on people. Or was it God? They even had a project to visit the West African country. Felix was so proud of his fatherland. He was a French speaker and would use French expressions from time to time. He would go on and on about his native country.

Keisha was fascinated and drawn to the country and its culture. She had always wanted to visit it but it was not meant to be. Anyway, she had to snap out of her thoughts. This was all in the past. Although she admitted that she could not erase a whole part of her daughter's history. After all, Tanya was half-Cameroonian too, just like Zack. That was at least one thing they had in common. He may be in a better position to understand her as a result.

"Are you familiar with Cameroonian music?" Zack asked as he joined her again.

"Yes, we used to listen to a lot of Makossa."

Zack had told her he always liked good music. But he was mostly drawn to the gospel genre. Although he would occasionally listen to jazz music.

"Oh really? I'm more familiar with Manu Dibango. He was famous for his afrobeat and afro-jazz style of music. Unfortunately, he died of COVID-19 earlier this year," Zack replied.

"Oh, that's sad. I vaguely remember him being mentioned but I can't think of where I heard his name."

"At least, he lived his life to the fullest.

It was also uncanny how her daughter was drawn to Cynthia. It was as if she had picked it up unconsciously, without realising that they somehow had something in common. She wasn't sure whether it was a good thing or a bad thing. But she prayed that everything would turn out well for everyone involved.

They all went to the restaurant for a meal.

"Mum, how long are we staying at Grandad Clive and Grandma Cynthia's?"

She had started calling them Grandma and Grandad. Keisha had mixed feelings about it. Nothing was going on between her and Zack, not yet anyway. Yet Clive and Cynthia had adopted them as family. Once again, Zack came to her rescue. "You'll stay as long as it is necessary."

"That's great!"

"You like staying with them, don't you?"

"Oh yes!"

"And why is that?"

"Grandma Cynthia is always cooking lovely food."

"That's true, you know," added Keisha.

"But I also like playing with Dylan, Evan, and André. They love hearing my Bible stories."

"Jack and Sara told me that they were asking after you. They wanted to come and visit my parents to see you," Zack said, smiling.

"I always wanted to have younger brothers and sisters," Tanya said innocently.

Keisha felt embarrassed and did not know where to look.

"How many would you like?" asked Zack.

"A brother and sister."

"Fair enough," he answered.

He wanted Keisha to realise that Tanya was not opposed to her starting a new relationship and even having a new family. At least Keisha could not use Tanya as an excuse for not allowing him into their lives. He was very satisfied with the turn of the conversation. Keisha, on the other hand, didn't know what to do with herself.

"Would you like something else to drink, Tanya?" asked Keisha, trying to divert the conversation.

"No, I'm okay, Mum. Thank you."

"Hey, there goes Jay," Clive said, waving at him. Jay approached the table.

"How are you keeping, Jay? Do you care to join us?"

"I'm having something to eat with some members of the choir later on. But I would love some coffee."

"So, what have you been doing with yourself? We came back from our trip and you were nowhere to be found."

"Well, it's a long story, Cynthia. But that's all in the past. By the way, thanks for recommending me for the job, Clive," he answered, realising that they were not aware of what had happened. He was not about to discuss it with them. But little did he know that the whole thing will burst open later on anyway. And there was not much he could do to stop it from happening.

"No worries. My pleasure. You have a massive talent. My son's choir needed it. And here we are today!"

"Yes, we're delighted to have him indeed," Zack said.

***

Julie was watching them from afar, fuming. How did this happen? She could not help but feel envious. "My plans have failed miserably. Keisha is even getting very close to Zack's family. I'm so annoyed about the whole thing," she mused aloud. It looked like she had actually brought the two of them together. And she was going to do everything in her power to prevent this from going further.

"Hello. So, what are you doing here?" Linda was asking Julie.

She jumped, as she was taken by surprise. She had not expected Linda to be right behind her.

"Nothing," she answered briefly and a bit too fast, sounding as if she was caught off guard or doing something bad.

"I remember your face, but I can't quite remember your name."

"I'm Julie. I'm part of the Abundant Life Ministries choir."

"Oh yes, I remember now. You're part of Zack's choir."

"That's right."

The look on Linda's face said she suspected Julie was up to something. "So how are you feeling about the whole thing?"

"You mean the competition?"

"Yes, what do you think?"

"Well, we'll just have to wait and see."

Julie didn't trust Linda, and the feeling was mutual.

Linda moved on from where she was and Julie watched her approach a stranger.

"Hello, can I help you?"

"I'm alright, thank you."

Detective Slim did not want to be detected.

Chapter XIII | The Night before the First Audition

Well before the rest of the team came down, Jay found himself in the lobby. He was feeling optimistic. This was going to be his time to shine. He had got the break he needed. Doors were opening for him at long last. He was going to be famous. He had moved from ministry to ministry but had never been given the chance to prove himself. It felt good that the song they were going to use in the competition was written when he was at his lowest, and now it was going to bring joy to others. Everyone had liked it, and he was delighted that they had treated it with respect. He felt validated and smiled at the thought of all the ministries that had kicked him out. They would regret not having kept him in their choir, he mulled. He felt like he was on top of the world. He just hoped he had succeeded in conquering some of his demons.

***

Julie had quickly freshened up and was making her way to the lobby. She also had issues with Jay. But then everyone in the choir was wary of her. She was a difficult person. She felt entitled and had this sense that he had taken what rightfully belonged to her. She was really frustrated because she had not got anything she had wanted so far. Zack had no interest in her and everyone seemed to have put the recent little scandal with Keisha behind them. She had still not found the husband she was looking for. All in all, it was a difficult time for her. And she didn't get to be the lead singer; she felt hard done by.

In her opinion, there was some favouritism going on towards Jay. But she had a strong impression that he was not being fully transparent. She was uneasy when she was around him. She could not quite put her finger on it.

Her intuition was telling her that there was something he was hiding and she had every intention of discovering what it was. Who knows, she might be able to use it against him. She decided to get closer to Jay to find out more about him, to know what was up with him.

***

"Hi, Jay, are you going to the hotel restaurant for something to eat?"

"I'm just waiting for the rest of the group."

"If you're not quick, there won't be any tables left."

Just then, they heard someone calling Jay.

"Hey, Jay!!! I can't believe it, man! How have you been?"

Jay seemed shocked and immediately looked troubled. What on earth was Roger doing in the hotel?

"Hey, Roger, what are you doing here?"

"I'm part of the organising team for a singing competition. And you?"

"I'm the lead singer in our church choir, we're taking part in the competition."

"Cool… It's great to see you, it's been a while."

Jay didn't know what to say. Julie was listening attentively and could see there was something fishy about Jay's reaction. Roger looked delighted, even ecstatic, to see Jay and could not keep his eyes off him. In contrast, Jay's heart was sinking. He thought he had left his demons far behind him; he did not know they were going to come back to haunt him so quickly. He was trying very hard to avoid looking at Roger. Tom and Fiona, along with members of the Victory Church Choir from Edinburgh, joined them and started asking questions about the competition.

"The big question on everyone's lips is, who are the panel members?" Tom said.

"I'm not supposed to tell you this. It's confidential. So keep it to yourselves. There are four panel members: Annette Rimes, you know, the famous Award-winning singer and songwriter; Sean Carter, the renowned TV music producer; gospel artist and Dove Award winner Divine; and the Choir of the Year leader from years back, Nick Smith."

"Wow, that's pretty impressive!" exclaimed Fiona.

"What a line-up," said Julie.

For once, she wasn't being blasé.

"Can you tell us: what's the trend? What are they looking for this year? I know that last year they were looking for a new sound. The previous year it was more about classic hymns, but what about this year?" Tom wanted to know.

"I know that they're looking for originality this time around."

"That's good to know. I think we stand a good chance with our songs then," Julie said to Jay.

Jay did not respond. His mind was elsewhere; other things were troubling him. How was he going to get rid of Roger? He shivered at the thought of Roger running his mouth. There were things he did not want shared. He was desperate to leave his past behind him.

***

Roger had no intention of going anywhere. He was waiting for the right time to have a private chat with Jay.

"Shall we go to the pub next door? The food is pretty decent and not too pricey."

He planned to get some drinks in as well, but he knew better than to mention it. He wanted it to be a fait accompli. He had to get Jay at all costs.

The Fisherman's Cabin was the name of the pub. It was famous for its fish and chips. On Thursday nights they usually had a band playing. Tonight, there was country music.

"How do you know each other?" asked Julie.

"We met years ago," answered Jay, obviously a bit too vaguely for Julie's liking.

"Where?" insisted Julie.

"We were once part of the same choir."

"Really?"

"Yes, but I'd rather not talk about it," Jay said.

"Let's have some drinks," Roger suggested, knowing that it would be a welcome distraction for Jay, but it could also set his plan in motion nicely.

That's when the drinking started. Roger offered a round of drinks to the small group. One thing led to another and before long, they were all slightly drunk. Julie had seen enough to form a pretty good idea of the nature of the relationship between Jay and Roger. By the end of the evening, Roger was not even pretending any longer. He could not care less and felt that he had nothing to hide.

Julie decided to make her exit and go back to her room; she did not want to be exhausted the next day. How could she use this information to her advantage? She had to think about this carefully. This time around, she did not want to mess things up.

Roger, Jay, Tom, and Fiona could not stop drinking.

***

Tom and Fiona stayed and started posting funny photos and information about the competition on Facebook, Instagram, TikTok, Twitter, and WhatsApp. They were completely oblivious to the agreement they had signed a few hours earlier. It caught the attention of MSN UK and Google news immediately. Before long, it had inundated the internet. By the morning, millions would have seen the postings.

The MBN Senior Management got wind of the fact that details of the competition had been leaked. The executives were livid; they had wanted to break the news in the national media and television. The exclusive photos and interviews would have brought in welcomed financial manna for the network, particularly following the impact of the lockdown. They contacted the choir leaders and summoned all of the participants to an urgent meeting first thing the next morning.

***

Cynthia and Clive were enjoying their time with Zack, Keisha, and Tanya. They had just finished eating.

"Mum, can I go and spend time with Michelle and Caroline?"

They had also come with their parents.

"It's quite late, Tanya."

"But I don't feel like sleeping right now."

"Tanya, just go to your room and we'll see you tomorrow. It's going to be a long day and you'll have plenty of time to enjoy yourself with your friends."

"Tanya, let's go. Your mum and Zack still have things to sort out for tomorrow. Come on," Cynthia said with a big smile.

Tanya had no choice but to go with them. She got up and said goodnight to both her mother and Zack. Keisha felt shy the moment she was left alone with Zack.

"Shall we go for a walk?"

"Alright."

She was eager to leave the restaurant as she was concerned that the rest of the choir would see them. She did not want to fuel any more rumours.

They walked down by the canal. It was a quiet and pleasant night and there was a light breeze – ideal for a stroll by the river Thames.

"Keisha, I wanted us to be alone because I need to tell you something."

She held her breath, too afraid to look at him.

"I have feelings for you, and I can't get you out of my mind. I have been trying to fight them off, but the more I try, the more the feelings persist. I think about you all the time. I'm looking for a serious relationship. I would eventually like to settle down and start a family. I believe we are right for each other." He spoke very fast and was looking at her intently.

Keisha was in a state of panic as she had not seen this coming. Zack could sense her fear.

"I don't want you to feel pressured to answer," he said quickly. "In fact, I want us to pray about this. I will pray and I want you to do the same, to see if this will work. I know you were badly hurt in the past. I will never hurt you and will do everything in my power to make you happy. But I want us to bring this to God in prayer."

"I would be lying if I said I didn't feel anything for you. I do. I also like that you have faith in God and always involve Him in everything you do. But I do need some time, Zack."

"I know, but I just had to make my intentions known."

"I appreciate that. But you know, as you said, I had a bad experience in the past."

While she thought it might be a good thing for Tanya, because of the connection with Cameroon, she was not sure about it being good for her. Her past experience made her reluctant to get involved with someone again. 'Once bitten, twice shy' was the expression that came to mind.

"Yes, but I'm different. I'm not like your ex-husband. I will never hurt you, Keisha."

"That's what they always say at the beginning."

"I will always love you with all my heart, Keisha."

He was hurt that she would compare him with her former husband. But he also knew that it was understandable to think like that after a bad experience.

"I've heard all this before you know. I got hurt so badly, it's hard for me to trust again. I'm just being real with you."

"You can trust me, Keisha. All I want is to make you happy. I want to see you smile. I want you to be the mother of my kids. I want us to spend the rest of our lives together."

"Well, I'm not sure I'm the right person."

"You said that you feel something for me."

"Yes, but…"

"Are you going to throw all of that away because of something that happened in the past? Give love a chance. Once again…"

"I don't know…"

"Don't think about it. Just open your heart to me."

He was trying everything he could to convince her. She did not know how long she could hold out.

"But that's the thing. I did open my heart one time and regretted it."

"Don't you want to take another risk? Don't you want another opportunity to love?"

"I don't know," Keisha answered helplessly. She could not help her feelings of fear and doubt. "I have so much going on at the moment. Some issues that need resolving. I think it's the wrong time for me to start anything right now."

"Will you at least pray about it? In fact, I would love us to pray about it right here and then we can do so separately as well."

They held hands and prayed together. Keisha felt at peace, no longer shy or self-conscious. Zack, on the other hand, had mixed feelings. He needed herculean self-control. At least she had not rebuffed him or fled. But he had wanted more. However, he knew that he needed to be extremely patient or else he ran the risk of losing her altogether, for good. And that was something he was not prepared to go through.

***

Alex Lynch, an executive at the MBN, was calling his mobile phone. Alex was Zack's contact and he knew immediately that something was wrong.

"Hi, Alex."

"Did you hear what happened?" He did not even respond to Zack's greetings.

"No, what are you talking about?" Zack was alarmed. He hoped that it had nothing to do with one of the guys in his choir.

"There's some d***, excuse my English, who messed up badly. They leaked some information about the competition. It's splashed all over the internet."

"It's not one of my guys, is it?"

"No, it was two participants from another choir, not sure which one."

"That's good to hear," Zack said, relieved. "I mean, it's good that it's not one of us."

"You and your choir should come down to the reception by 8:45 a.m. tomorrow. Let them know straight away."

Zack posted to the WhatsApp group to notify them all of the morning meeting. He also asked for a general meeting straight afterwards. The choir needed to have a prayer meeting.

***

Later on that night, Tanya was having a nightmare. This time she was not dreaming of a Bible character. She saw a man chasing after her mum. He had a gun and he was trying to kill her.

Fortunately, she managed to hide. The man was looking for her but could not find her. Suddenly, Zack appeared. He rescued Keisha and brought her to a safe place. Tanya woke up and went to her mum's room.

"Mum, I just had a nightmare."

She began to relate the dream to her mother.

"Just go back to sleep, Tee. Don't worry about it. It's just a nightmare."

"Yeah, but I think it means that Zack is a good guy, Mum. I think God is trying to show us that he won't harm us. On the contrary, he will protect us from the bad guys. We will be safe with him. You have nothing to fear, Mum."

"How are you so sure?"

"I think that's what the dream means."

"Well, we'll have to see."

"Come on, Mum."

"That's alright, Tee. Zack and I are just friends."

"I would love him as the father I have never had, Mum."

"Really? You're going a bit fast, aren't you? How do you know that he likes or even loves me?"

"I can tell he really likes you. He's always looking at you."

"Wow, Miss Tee, you seem to have observed him a lot!"

"It's so obvious, Mum. Everybody, except you, has noticed it."

"Noticed what?"

"Mum, come on, stop pretending," Tanya said with exasperation.

Tanya went back to sleep. Keisha was pensive. Could Tanya's interpretation of the dream be true? Could she really trust Zack? She had been disappointed in the past; left to gather the pieces of her shattered life. It was a long and painful process. She was able to overcome her hurtful divorce, but she was not ready to go through another ordeal. She promised herself to be careful around Zack.

"Sweet dreams, Tanya," her mother said, still thinking about her daughter's words. Just as she was about to close her eyes and her guard was down, she thought that Zack could be a good man that she could trust. He might be the one; who knows?

Chapter XIV | Meeting Divine

Fiona and Tom were still hungover from the previous night. They vaguely remembered some of what had happened at the pub. The only thing they knew for certain was that they had been summoned to the lobby for a meeting far too early for their liking. After all, the auditions did not start until two o'clock.

The two MBN executives – Alex Lynch and Peter Nichols – were present, flanked by Agnieszka and Linda. They were all looking sombre. Even Linda had lost her smile. They waited for the latecomers to arrive.

"Last night, some of you breached the agreement that was signed yesterday. Would the people who posted online pictures and information about this competition step forward, please?"

No one uttered a word. Everyone was looking at each other. Some were aware of the mishap, whilst others did not have a clue.

"Okay, since nobody is brave enough to take responsibility for what they have done, we will have to expose you. Will Fiona Gordon and Tom Fraser come forward?"

The two culprits looked at each other in disbelief and moved towards the front of the crowd.

"This is totally unacceptable behaviour," continued Alex. "This sole act of irresponsibility will have devastating consequences for us. We have no choice but to sanction you and expel you from the competition. You will have to leave with immediate effect. You will also have to delete any photos from your phones. You will hear from us very soon. Go and collect your belongings and don't forget to leave your badges at the reception. Linda, please escort them to their rooms. For the rest of you, let this be a warning to you that we will not tolerate any nonsense from any of you," he said angrily.

Fiona burst into tears and ran out of the room. All the participants were left in shock. Some were of the opinion that the senior management decision was far too harsh. Others felt that it could harm the reputation of all church choirs, as there were certain standards expected of the members. But all they could do was to put the incident behind them and focus on the auditions that were to take place later that day.

From then on, they were all careful about giving any details to family members and loved ones until the winners were officially announced by the organisers. The Abundant Life choir then came together for prayer. Zack gave a little pep talk before they started praying.

"It is important to remember that we are Christians and we must act with integrity. You have to mind how you behave at all times and not bring shame to this ministry. We have to make our church proud of us. Remember that we have come here for a purpose, which is to win. Don't get carried away by other things. Don't be distracted. Stay focused. We can do this. Let us pray."

They had a one-hour prayer session and everyone felt a lot better and calmer afterwards.

***

Tanya had been wondering where Pearl had gone. They had not seen her in months, which was very unusual. Any time she tried to find out, her mum would act funny and send her away. She was convinced that something was definitely not right. All that was familiar and dear to her seemed to have gone: her nanny, their home, and some of her friends. There were a lot of strangers around and it could be quite intimidating. She did feel safe with Clive and Cynthia, however. She was also delighted to know that Pastor Ben had arrived in the morning with his parents. His mother was part of the choir.

"Hey, Pastor Ben."

"Hey, Tanya, how are you?"

"I'm fine, just a bit worried about Mum. She's acting a bit strange."

"What do you mean?"

"Well, she seems to be stressed. We're not staying at home but at uncle Zack's parents' house. My babysitter has disappeared; I don't know where she is. Usually, when my mum has to go somewhere, she will ask Pearl to come and mind me. A while ago, we went to the police and they kept my mum for a long time. I was so afraid. I thought she was going to prison. She's not been going to work either and I just don't understand what is going on."

To Tanya, the adult world was a very complicated one. She wished she could go back to when she was too young to understand what was going on around her.

"Anyway, people don't go to prison just like that. There has to be a reason, a motive. Did you try to ask her?"

"I tried several times but, you know, Mum would tell me to stop asking questions or send me away. I'm so worried."

"Don't worry. Always trust in God," said Pastor Ben. As usual, he sounded a lot older than his age. Tanya felt some comfort talking to him. It gave her some sense of normality as well.

"I find it hard to talk to Mum sometimes. When I ask her about my father, she gets angry. I also asked her why my eyes are blue when I'm black. She just says that it's how I was born and that I should be grateful to God that I wasn't born disabled."

"God created you like that," said Pastor Ben.

"But why am I so different? Sometimes I feel so awkward. I wish I was like everyone else."

"You shouldn't! You're special. You're not like all of us. At least you stand out; everyone notices you."

Tanya struggled so much with her appearance. She was still getting used to people staring at her. Sometimes people would make comments. Other kids would say: "Mum, look at her eyes, they are blue!" It made her feel awkward and self-conscious.

Tanya went to meet up with Michelle and Caroline, who had both come along with one of their parents. The girls decided to go round the hotel. They went for a walk in the little park between the hotel and the river Thames. They found gospel singer Divine, sitting on a bench. They were shocked to see that she was smoking! They looked at each other, not knowing what to think. They elbowed each other.

"Look, isn't that Divine, sitting on the bench?"

"I'm not sure. Is she not a Christian? How come she's smoking?"

"Well, I'm sure that's Divine. I would recognise her anywhere."

They walked over and stood in front of her.

"Hi, are you Divine?"

"Yeah, I am." She threw her cigarette into the nearby bin.

"We are big fans of yours."

"Is that so?"

"Yes, we love the way you sing."

"What are you doing here?"

"We came with our parents. They are taking part in the competition."

"Which choir is that? No, no don't tell me. I don't want to know. I need to remain neutral and not have any sort of connection with members of the choirs and their entourage. So best you don't tell me."

"You have very strict rules."

"Yes, you can say that again. I don't want to be ruled out of the competition as one of the panellists. But I could do with some company. Would you girls like something to eat?"

They were not sure at first, but thought there was nothing wrong with going with Divine. It was not every day that they would come across a star.

"Oh yes, we would love to," said Caroline on behalf of all three girls.

This stay was turning out to be exciting, as they had not expected this at all. What a nice surprise! They would have a story to tell their family, friends, and the people in church.

"We could go for a bite to eat. What's a typical English meal?" Divine enquired.

"Fish and chips!" Michelle and Caroline said in unison.

"You have to have salt and vinegar on the chips and a bit of tartar sauce on the side."

"Chips with vinegar? That's sounds—"

"It's yummy," interrupted Tanya enthusiastically. "Just give it a try and you will agree."

"Okay, let's go for it!"

Divine did enjoy the fish and chips with salt and vinegar. "It's a little unusual but surprisingly tasty," she said.

"We have it every Friday night. It's a tradition."

"We tend to have fish and chips on Saturday nights," said Caroline.

"We eat it whenever we feel like it," commented Tanya.

"Tell us, Divine, when did you start singing?" Caroline was the extrovert and the most outspoken and inquisitive of the bunch.

"I started singing as a child in my church choir. I was also the choir leader as a teen. They were the good times. Life was less complicated."

"Why?" asked Caroline.

"Oh well, I have a lot of responsibilities as an adult, as a Christian. People expect so much of me."

Divine was talking to herself. She was happy to be in London, as she was free to be herself. She did not have to be Miss Perfect. No pretence. No mask. She knew she should not smoke, but she could not help it. The last tour was so stressful she found herself chain-smoking. She had asked God to take it away many times, but time and again, she would fall flat out. She still believed that one day God would answer her prayer.

***

Tanya got the fright of her life. She had been feeling funny for a few hours. Her tummy was sore and was making some movements, so she went to the toilet. She almost fainted when she saw blood dripping down the toilet seat and even down her legs. She could not believe it. What should she do?

"Tanya, what are you doing in there?" Caroline was shouting at the top of her voice, and banging on the door.

There was no answer.

"Are you coming out?" continued Caroline

"Wait, there's something wrong." Michelle knew that this was very unlike Tanya.

"Are you alright, Tanya?"

"What's going on? Open the door."

"I can't, there's something wrong."

Caroline looked at Michelle and suddenly understood.

"Tanya, do you have your periods?"

"Yes, yes," she answered hesitantly.

"Okay, that's alright, it's nothing to worry about. Open the door."

There was silence.

"Yes, open the door," she repeated

Tanya opened the door, hesitantly, after a few minutes. Michelle held her.

Just before she could answer, Divine walked into the toilets.

"What is going on in here, girls, you've been in here forever!"

"Tanya just had her first period."

"Really? You poor thing," she said as if it was a disease, which made things worse for Tanya. But she quickly tried to comfort her.

"Don't worry, it just shows that you've just become a woman, that's all."

"I, I'm a bit embarrassed," said Tanya with a sigh of relief.

"Don't be silly, it's nothing to be ashamed of

***

Divine was fascinated by Tanya's blue eyes and black skin. It was so unusual. She realised she had a soft spot for her as she felt a connection with Tanya. She also knew that this was not a chance meeting. This meeting was divine; she pondered, laughing in her heart at the play on words.

"It's a good thing I have some pads in my bag; let me get a couple for you. You will have to use one and get changed once you get back to the hotel."

***

Keisha was in her hotel room, lying on the bed. She was thinking about Zack. The more she tried to suppress her feelings, the stronger they became. She missed him when he was absent. She did not know what to do with herself when he was there. The more she tried to forget about him, the more she thought about him. It was frustrating at times. But it was also exciting. She could feel her adrenaline going through the roof when he looked, spoke to, or smiled at her. She needed to be careful; she did not want to be hurt again. *Oh, Lord, what shall I do?*

Just then, her mobile phone rang. It was Pam calling, an old friend who she had kept in touch with from her Imperial College days. They were roommates in the Marie Curie Hall. She had been working overseas and had dedicated her time to working for international organisations, focusing on her career.

"How have you guys been? How is Tanya doing?"

"Hello, stranger!" she answered. "So good to hear from you. We're both fine. Where are you?"

"You won't believe it. I'm in Australia."

"What are you doing there?"

"Well, love brought me here."

"What? Pam, the career woman, in love?!?"

"That's right. It's happened! He is an Aussie. That's why I'm down under."

"I can't believe it, I'm so shocked."

"You'd better believe it. We're getting married next year."

"This is serious then."

"I've never been this serious in my life. That's the reason I'm calling you."

"I'm so happy for you!"

She felt a pinch in her heart. What was happening to her? She was happy for her friend, but she couldn't help feeling envious and she couldn't explain why. Maybe she envied Pam's courage. Or maybe she felt a bit jealous that her friend was tying the knot after a series of failed relationships, while she had not had a single relationship since she got divorced.

"Have you left your job in Dubai?" she asked.

"No, I'm on annual leave."

"So, tell me about him."

"He is in the same field as me. He works as a Petroleum Engineer project manager. That's how we met."

"Office romance, hey?"

"This is not just a fling. We're both in love. I know he is the one."

Keisha was truly amazed and intrigued. This was a facet of her friend's personality that she had never seen before. It was actually refreshing to see her like this.

"I'm hoping that you guys will be able to make it."

She remembered how Pam had been there in her darkest hours as if it was yesterday. She had put up with her depression. Had helped with minding Tee. She was there for them.

"Yes, we will try to be there."

"I would love you guys to attend my wedding. It would mean so much to me, to us. I told Gary about you guys. He can't wait to meet you two."

"I'll do everything in my power to be there, my dear. We would not miss it for anything in the world."

"I'm glad to hear that!"

"Who else do I know that will be going?"

"Of course, my parents and siblings, Mary Nichols, Hans Christensen who is coming from Germany where I moved to after graduating, Nathan O'Carroll, and Noriko is coming over from Japan. That's all I can think of right now."

"I haven't seen them in years. Over a decade, I'd say. It's an opportunity for a reunion."

"Of course, the wedding taking place so far from the shores of Britain might mean that some friends will not be able to come. But that's why I'm giving people lots of notice."

"What date is the wedding?"

"The 18th of August. We figured that it's the summer holidays, so most people should be free to attend."

"Are you going to relocate to Australia?"

"Not for the time being. We will keep on working in Dubai till the end of our contracts. Then, we will decide whether we want to settle in Australia or the United Kingdom."

After she hung up, it made Keisha think. This was food for thought. Even Pam had made the jump. But then, she was a risk-taker. That's just the way she was. They always used to joke that she had itchy feet, as she could never stay in one place for long. She would say that she was a free spirit, a nomad at heart. She could never commit to a relationship because all she cared about was work, travelling, and meeting new people, without any strings attached. Her sudden turnaround was amazing. It made her reflect on her own situation. She was a coward. She had to face her fears once for all, but did not know how. She had to move on. How do you erase a painful past just like that? She could not let the past, no matter how horrible, rob her of her present and her future.

Chapter XV | First Auditions

"**M**um, guess what? I just had my periods!" Keisha stayed silent. Shoot, she had completely forgotten to have that conversation with her daughter.

"I'm so sorry, Tee, I completely forgot to have a talk on this you and I. It completely went out of my mind. There's been so much going on."

"No worries, Mum."

Keisha felt a bit bad. She had been too absorbed by her own issues. She made it a point to set aside some one-to-one time for a chat with Tanya at the weekend. She understood Tanya's annoyance and felt bad about it. She had let her daughter down this time around and knew she was at fault. She would not only do her periods education, but her sex education too. Now that Tanya had passed the childhood stage, she needed to make her aware of the implications.

Tanya knew that it was very unlike her mum, who was usually very attentive and a real mother hen. But lately, she had been very absent-minded. Tanya felt like their lives had been turned upside down and she had no idea why.

***

Right now, Keisha had to prepare for the auditions. She needed some time to think before the competition kicked off. Their slot had fallen later that afternoon. Tanya went for a little nap. She fell into a deep, disquieted sleep. She started dreaming of the Prophet Elisha and the Shunammite woman's son. She had shown great hospitality to the prophet and even set a room aside for his visits. The woman had been childless for a long time and her husband was old.

"About this time next year, you will hold a son in your arms," Prophet Elisha told her.

"No, my Lord!" she objected. "Please, man of God, don't mislead your servant."

She eventually conceived a child the following year, about the same time as was spoken by the prophet. Her son grew, and one day he went to his father, who was with the reapers.

"My head! My head!" he said to his father.

The father said to his servants, "Carry him to his mother."

He was brought to his mother, laid on her lap, and then he died.

She rushed to the man of God, taking one of the servants with her. She met him at Mount Carmel and took hold of his feet. Elisha's servant, Gehazi, wanted to push her away.

But the servant of God said, "Leave her alone! She is in bitter distress, but the Lord has hidden it from me and has not told me why."

"Did I ask for a son, my Lord? Did I not say 'Do not deceive me?'" the Shunammite said to him. Elisha told Gehazi, "Tuck your cloak into your belt, take my staff in hand, and run. Don't greet anyone you meet, and if anyone greets you, do not answer. Lay my staff on the boy's face."

But the child's mother said, "As surely as the Lord lives and as your soul lives, I will not leave you."

So, he got up and followed her. Gehazi had gone ahead and laid the staff on the boy's face, but there was no sound or response. So Gehazi went back to meet Elisha and told him, "The boy has not awakened."

Elisha went to the room where the boy was lying on the couch. He went in, shut the door on the two of them, and prayed to the Lord. Then he laid on the boy, mouth to mouth, eyes to eyes, hands to hands. The boy's body grew warmer as he stretched himself out on him. He walked back and forth, and then he stretched out on him once more; the boy sneezed seven times and opened his eyes.

Just then, Keisha was trying to wake Tanya up.

"Wakey, wakey, Tee. It's time to wake up. Before we go for the first auditions, I would like to have a chat with you, love."

"What about?"

"First of all, I'm so sorry for not having an in-depth conversation about this before now."

"Oh, don't worry about that."

"I know that menstrual health is now compulsory at school this year. But it's my fault. I should have realised that your menstruation could come before you received periods education. I just didn't think it through."

"It's alright, Mum, I knew a little about it." she said, half-joking.

"I brought my laptop so that we can watch a Period Education programme together. That way we can have a conversation about it. If you have any questions, you can ask me and we will pause the video."

Keisha wanted to do things properly this time around and make up for her negligence. They watched the story of thirteen-year-old Thelma who spoke about how she did not have the money to buy any period products. She panicked and did not know what to do. As a result, she could not go to school for days. Apparently, this situation was not uncommon in the United Kingdom.

"Is that true, Mum?"

"Yes, I read somewhere that over forty per cent of girls cannot afford to buy them."

Tanya, always full of compassion, felt bad for these girls. She was truly touched by Thelma's story. The kind-hearted daughter wanted to make a donation to the charity taking care of girls in Thelma's situation.

"Why do girls have periods and not boys?"

"Periods mark the end of childhood and the beginning of childbearing ability for a girl."

This was the best and simplest way she could explain it to Tanya without being too technical about it.

"You have to understand that if you have a sexual relationship with a lad, you may become pregnant."

"Really?"

She was still so innocent. Keisha looked at her daughter. Her baby girl was becoming a beautiful young woman right in front of her eyes.

"Yes, that's right."

Tanya thought this was serious. She had no intention of becoming a mother any time soon, so boys were off-limits from now on, apart from Pastor Ben. She was happy that her mother had taken the time to watch the programme with her and answer her questions.

***

Detectives Kelleher and Slim were waiting at the reception. They were trying to be inconspicuous. They had to take multiple trips to the bar, toilets, restaurant, and the park to avoid detection and had gained some information by snooping around. Detective Slim got talking to Linda, who opened up easily. She thought that Detective Slim was cute and friendly. She had noticed him when the choirs first arrived at the hotel.

"What is going on in here?"

This was just an icebreaker and a way to start a conversation with her. He knew exactly what was going on. She did not mind at all.

"It's a gospel competition. There are twenty choirs from all over the United Kingdom. We're about to start. The first auditions are taking place this afternoon over at the MBN studios."

"Where is that?"

"Over at Canary Wharf."

"I would love to attend these sessions, you know." He gave her a very charming smile as he could see she had a soft spot for him. She was obviously not ready to see him go anyway.

"I could get you a good spot for the auditions. As part of the organising team, I have extra tickets."

He had to keep Detective Kelleher posted about the latest developments. They agreed that she would stay in the car and also keep the boss informed. They would have to stay put around the hotel and the MBN studios for the next couple of days.

***

All the choirs were present at the reception in the MBN building. They were given the programme for the afternoon and saw that the auditions would take a total of two and a half hours. After an hour of deliberations, the choirs going through to the next round would be announced at around 5.30 p.m. The Abundant Life Choir was somewhere in the middle of the auditions.

There were more dramas during the auditions. Annette Rimes could not make it due to a COVID-19 scare. She was replaced by British chart-topper Lauren Hicks.

Some choirs experienced mishaps. The choir from Brighton unfortunately sang off-key. The choir from Peterborough experienced some technical issues with their microphones and instruments and had to restart a couple of times, which was stressful for them. This affected the group who gave a bland performance. But the biggest drama yet was with the choir from Kent. As the choir was performing, a man came over to where the panel members were and said something to them. The choir members were wondering what was going on.

"Who is Amanda Mills?" asked Nick.

There was no answer.

"Will Amanda Mills step forward, please?" asked Nick for the second time. This time his voice was louder.

Amanda eventually made her way towards the front of the choir and stood before the judges.

"We've just got a report that you tested positive for the COVID-19 virus."

"That's not true."

"Well, we just got a report from an anonymous member of the public that you recently tested positive for the disease. Is it true?"

"No, I haven't. It's not true."

"Unfortunately, we cannot take any risks. You and the whole choir will not be able to perform, I'm afraid."

"Oh no," cried Amanda. "I did a test that can show that I'm negative, but I don't have it with me. I left it at home in Kent."

"Well, I'm sorry, but I have to follow the orders. There's nothing anyone can do at this stage. For health and safety reasons, you and the entire choir will have to retire from the competition, because you could expose us to the virus. People will do anything at times to get what they want, including lie to take part in this sort of competition. We have no way of confirming if you have recently had the virus or not.

"To keep everyone safe, you and the choir will have to make your way back to the hotel and go home. We're sorry that this has happened. It's unfortunate, but our hands are tied. Also, you are going to have to get back to us with your results as soon as you get home tonight so that we know your status and where we stand as a whole. Can you do that for us?"

"Yes, I will," whispered Amanda. She was in a terrible state, crying profusely. She felt really bad for the choir and could not help but feel guilty too.

Some choir members gathered around her, trying to comfort her. They left the stage and went back to the hotel.

Everyone was shaken and knew that there was a risk that they had been exposed to the virus if the story turned out to be true. The organisers took the view that they had to try to save the competition. They saw it best to sacrifice the choir involved so as not to have to send everyone home. The Abundant Life choir gave a stellar performance and the judges thought that they were top of the crop.

***

Meanwhile, Detective Slim was carrying on with his investigation. He had managed to get close to Keisha's choir. Who was talkative enough to give him the information he needed? The difficulty was that Keisha was a private person, from what he could gather. Nobody was readily available to talk. Or so he thought until he encountered Julie complaining about Keisha.

"That Keisha, she thinks she's all that and more."

"Why do you say that?" Detective Slim asked her.

"She acts like she's a saint, yet she's sleeping around." She knew it was not true, but she could not help dishing the dirt on her.

"Who with?"

"Well, the other day, she was caught red-handed with Zack. Literally living together, imagine!"

"Zack? The choir leader, right?"

"Yes!"

"Are they going out together?"

"Well, what do you think? Is that not obvious to you?!?"

"Is she staying at Zack's place?"

"No, she and her daughter now live with Zack's parents."

"Why is that?"

"Wooo! You do ask a lot of questions, don't you?"

"Well, I just like to know about others, that's all," he said with a mischievous smile.

"So, you're, kind of nosy shall we say…" replied Julie with an ironic smile. Always the suspicious kind, she was wondering if there was more to him than met the eye. However, if there was one thing she liked doing was gossiping.

"Just curious, that's all."

"Well, like I was saying, people think she's all that. But they don't know who she truly is."

"What do you mean?"

"Well, she killed her son, apparently."

"Really?" Detective Slim was taken aback. They did not have that information. Their investigation had not revealed that. Was Keisha some kind of psychopath that had managed to escape the attention of the police? He had to let Detective Kelleher know so that she could do some investigating on their laptop in the car while she was waiting for him to finish up. Well, the plot was getting more and more interesting by the day. But they were far from resolving the case and already the big boss was putting pressure on them, stating that they were not on holiday, but on assignment.

"What about her daughter? What's her name again?" He pretended he could not remember so as not to raise her suspicion.

"Tanya? What about her? She's always hanging around Pastor Ben or the girls."

"Pastor Ben?"

"Oh, that's just his nickname, his real name is Ben. Apparently, it's like he swallowed the whole Bible up. He's always quoting Bible verses, even though he is just a teenager."

"Who are the girls?"

"Michelle and Caroline. She spends her time with them when they're in church."

Detective Slim kept this at the back of his mind. It was time for him to get moving. Otherwise, Julie's suspicions might grow stronger. He had to try to find Tanya. Maybe she might give them more clues as to what happened the night of the murder.

***

At 5.30 p.m., the participants all gathered on the main stage in the MBN studios. Everyone was waiting in anticipation. Zack was slightly nervous, wondering if their hard work had paid off.

Sean Carter stepped forward. "We are pleased to announce the choirs that are moving on to the next stage. The other members of the panel and myself agree that the quality of the performances we have seen today was astounding. It made it difficult for us to choose, but we had to make some hard decisions. We have decided that the following choirs will be going to the second audition."

Keisha was also very emotional; she knew what it meant for Zack and really wanted the choir to go to the next level. Jay's heart was pounding so hard. He was sweating. Julie wanted them to be selected, but it would not mean the same for her as she was not the lead singer. Then, they heard it: "Abundant Life Choir from London, you are through to the next round of auditions."

"Yeeessss!" shouted Jay, lifting his fist in the air as a sign of victory.

They all jumped, full of joy. Zack's parents, Tanya, and the children of the members of the choir joined in the celebrations. It was quite an achievement. They all hugged each other. Although they tried to keep to the social distancing, it was hard.

Detective Slim took advantage of the euphoria to mingle with the choir. He was trying to get close to Keisha and her friends.

***

They all went to a pub for a bistro meal. Zack had been avoiding Keisha. His feelings were so strong, but he did not want to give her the impression that he was forcing himself on her. She could sense that he was not his usual self. He was distant. She was sorry about it because she valued the time they spent together. She really liked talking to him and praying with him. She decided to make an effort.

"How do you feel about tomorrow?"

"I'm praying to God that we will win."

"We just have to do our best and God will do the rest," she said philosophically.

"Well, we need the favour of God. There are nine other choirs also praying like us, I'm sure." He laughed.

She enjoyed the fact that he did not hesitate to talk about God. She admired his strong faith. Zack had decided that he was not going to say a word about the last conversation they had. The ball was in her court and when she was ready, she would have to come to him and open up. After all, she was the one who said she needed time. He was not going to rush her, but this time around he wanted her to try a little harder.

Amanda Mills sent proof to the organisers as evidence that she did not have the virus. Unfortunately, this meant that her choir had paid a heavy price for what turned out to be a false accusation.

Chapter XVI | The Mirror Game

Early on Saturday morning, the second day of auditions, Divine went jogging. She needed to get away from the other panellists. They had big egos and were trying to outdo each other, which was not necessary. She could not be bothered with it all; it was all so childish! Nick was full of himself. He was the one who pushed for Amanda Mills and the rest of the choir to be kicked out of the competition. They did not even check where the information about Amanda came from or dig deeper to find out if it was even true. He also was trying to hit on Lauren; it was so ridiculous.

But what she could not stand was the fact that they had a profile of the kind of choir they were looking for. She just hated that. She liked being here in London, but she did not want to be part of this farce of a competition. They also seemed to want to pick an 'elite' choir from an established Anglican Church. She was not buying into it. Apart from herself, and maybe Sean, the other panellists just wanted a safe old-fashioned, traditional choir. She thought it was not fair at all. They should not be profiling; they should just be judging fairly.

"Hey, Divine!" shouted Tanya.

Divine was returning to the hotel after her little jog. Tanya was there with another boy.

"Hello, Tanya. How are you today? Are you feeling better?"

"When were you sick? What was wrong with you?" asked Pastor Ben, concerned.

"It's fine. Don't worry. I just wasn't a hundred per cent," said Tanya to avoid having to give him any more explanation than was necessary. She felt too embarrassed.

"What are you two doing here so early?"

"Pastor Ben and I were just talking…"

"About what?"

"The Lord Jesus Christ, the Bible, and the dreams that I sometimes have."

"I have to go," said Pastor Ben. "My parents will be looking for me. Bye, guys. See you later at the second auditions."

"Are you alright, Divine?"

***

Tanya felt that something was not right. She was a sensitive girl and could tell that Divine was not okay.

"I'm okay, Tanya," Divine was saying, obviously not wanting to share the reasons for her uneasiness. "What did your mum say when you told her about you having your periods?"

"Oh well, she felt bad, of course. I asked her why she never told me about it before. She could tell I wasn't happy."

"And what did she say?"

"Well, Mum has been worried lately, you know," she said, trying to defend her mother. Tanya paused for a moment. She could open up to Divine, she thought. She felt safe with the singer. She was like the big sister Tanya longed to have, although they were diametrically different. Divine was from Hawaii and had African American, Asian, and Caucasian ancestry, which gave her this exotic look. She could easily pass for a Miss

Universe, she was that beautiful to Tanya. Yet she was humble and compassionate, which is probably why she took the time to talk to Tanya. *She obviously knows I need someone to talk to and who can give me answers!*

"But Mum took the time to speak to me about it the other day. We even watched a Period Education programme together. We watched the story of Thelma. It made me realise that I've got it good compared to some others, you know. I will never be in a situation where I don't go to school because we're too broke to buy sanitary pads. Some girls even have to make their own pads. It's so sad."

"You're so generous, Tanya. Still thinking about someone else's pain and difficult situation.

"It's not that bad… Mum has been going through some stuff lately. Ever since Pearl disappeared out of our lives. She hasn't even been going to work."

"Who is Pearl?"

"My childminder. Any time I ask about her, Mum gets funny and sends me away. You'll never guess what happened."

"What?"

"We spent hours in the police station!"

"Why?"

"I have no idea. She just said it's nothing to worry about. Mum doesn't like to talk about a lot of things."

"Like what?"

"Like why I look the way I do."

"You mean your physical appearance?"

"Yes, my blues eyes and black skin. I get teased a lot about it at school."

"Oh, but you look so beautiful. You have amazing eyes. And the contrast with your skin is what makes you so striking."

"There was a bully in my class, well, when I used to go to school that used to call me all sorts of names. It caused me to lose my confidence."

"Don't let anyone put you down. You could be a model or an actress. Look, I have slanting eyes and I used to be teased a lot at school as well."

"What did you do?"

"Come, let's go to the toilets."

"What for?"

"Come on, just follow me. We're going to play what I call the mirror game."

They got to the hotel's empty toilets.

"Look at yourself in the mirror."

"Why?"

"Just do as I say… Say after me 'I'm fearfully and wonderfully made.'"

Tanya repeated her exact words.

"Say it to yourself, until you're convinced that these words of the Bible are true."

At first, she was unconvinced. It took her a while, but after some time, she began to believe. She felt as if a weight had been lifted from her shoulders.

"Wow, that was amazing!" She was impressed by the little exercise.

"There you go. That's great."

"How did you know to do that?"

"One day, one of my teachers, who was a Christian, took me to the bathroom and asked me to say exactly what I asked you to say. And I never looked back. You see, you have to accept yourself the way God made you. And God never makes a mistake."

For the first time in her life, Tanya looked at herself in the mirror and accepted herself the way she was. She felt good about herself. Her complexes and anxieties had subsided.

"Can I ask you a question?"

"Yes, of course. Go ahead!" Divine answered, not sure what to expect. Tanya was very inquisitive.

"Are you a Christian?"

"I grew up in church, so God has always been part of me."

"How come you smoke then?"

It's something that had shocked her as well as Michelle and Caroline. They could not get their heads around it. They had been taught not to drink alcoholic drinks or smoke. What they were unaware of was that she also regularly got drunk. But she was not about to tell Tanya that and make her even more disillusioned.

"Oh well, I was closer to God then than I am now."

"Why? What happened?" Tanya asked curiously.

"I've been hanging around with the wrong friends. The stress and anxiety at concerts and TV programmes took their toll on me, and one thing led to another. We all have our weaknesses, I guess. I got too busy with the music industry. I lost my way a bit and went astray. And here I am today." How could the singer be such an amazing and talented gospel artist and yet be so far from God? It was a mystery to Tanya. Adulthood was full of complexities.

"I've tried to beat it, but it's been getting the best of me."

"Why don't you ask the Lord to help you?"

"I have, but I have to keep on asking, I guess."

"Do you go to church?"

"I haven't had the time, 'cause I've been so busy."

Tanya was now disconcerted and concerned. She was wondering what kind of Christian Divine was.

***

As Tanya stared at her, Divine realised how unsettling the conversation had become. It was as though Tanya had made her hold a mirror up to herself and she realised how distant she had become from the Lord. She knew that things had to change. However, she also realised that the Lord had used her in Tanya's life as much as He had used the young girl to bless her. She felt much better now. And for the first time in years, she had that desire, that longing to rekindle her relationship with the Lord.

***

Detective Slim had been talking to Detective Kelleher about the latest events. They agreed he should continue mingling with the choir in order to get as much information as possible. They were surprised that no one had thought of asking him what he was doing at the competition and who he was with already. Detective Kelleher had dug through Keisha's past and found that she had killed her son by accident. It also meant that he had to be careful with any information Julie had fed him. She was clearly determined to badmouth Keisha at every opportunity. He put it down to jealousy and envy. But how could she go that far?

With his eagle eyes, he saw Divine and Tanya in the distance. He decided to get closer to the two and eavesdrop. He got some vital pieces of information, which left him with some questions. Why did she stop going to work? And why did she keep her daughter from going to school? Who was she running away or hiding from? They had to find out who her employer was. It was also interesting that Tanya had no idea that Pearl had died. He was not entirely sure why. It could be that Keisha wanted to protect her daughter from the pain. Or it could be something a lot more obscure. He saw them going to the toilets and decided to go back to their car and have a talk with his colleague.

Detective Kelleher was sitting in the car outside the hotel, keeping an eye on the hotel entrance.

"Can you do some research on Keisha?"

"What are you looking for?" asked Detective Kelleher.

"She hasn't been to work since the night of the murder. Four months is a long time to be in mourning for the murder of a nanny."

"Yes, indeed."

"Let's try to Google her name."

"Nothing is coming up…"

"You've got the wrong spelling, that's why. It's Keisha, not Kisha," corrected Detective Slim.

"Bingo! Got her on LinkedIn. Let's see what we've got here… She works at Dexter Pharmaceuticals as a Regulatory Manager. She's been there for years."

"Let's check their website as well. We need to find out about the management team and see who her boss is."

"Here we go. Here is the Regulatory Team. Let's see who's in charge of that department... There she is, her name is Claire McPherson."

"Right, we need to make arrangements to go there. But let's wait until the competition is over."

"How is it over there?" asked Detective Kelleher.

"Well, everyone is pretty excited, of course. It's the second round of auditions."

"What about Keisha's choir?"

"From what I hear, they stand a good chance."

"How do you know that?"

"Well, I used my famous charm and my amazing investigative skills," he said and grinned.

"What a wonder you are," stated Detective Kelleher, rolling her eyes theatrically. "But seriously, how do you know?"

"I got talking to some of the guys. Linda gave me some insights. I also heard some of the panellists saying that they were quite good. But then at this level, you would expect that."

"So, we should expect them to stay till the end then?"

"Yes, I think so."

"Oh dear, I'll just have to make the most of it all."

"Maybe you can also run a check on Zack Armstrong. He is the choir leader. Keisha seems to be close to him. Also, she and her daughter live at his parents' place. I'm curious as to why. Can you also do some searching on Julie? I'll text you her surname later. See if she comes up anywhere on social media: Facebook, Instagram, Twitter, TikTok, and the likes. Get me as much info as you can. Right, I'd better go back. You have your homework all set for you," he said, laughing.

***

Divine went back to the hotel. She met Shreya.

"Hello, Ms Wilson," she said with half a smile.

"Hello, Ms Gupta," she replied with a big smile.

"How was your morning jog?"

"It was great, thank you. See you later?"

Shreya did not answer. She was thinking of her poor mum. Her brother had called to say that their mother's state was getting worse by the day. She was extremely worried and had a hard time focusing on her job. Her absent-mindedness was being noticed by her colleagues. She even mixed up the rota, which is why she had to come to work that morning to cover for someone.

Divine went up to her hotel room. She thought she had not played the mirror game for herself in years. Maybe it was time to go back to her roots. Once she arrived in her room, she looked at herself in the mirror.

"I can do all things through Christ, who gives me strength. I can stop smoking and drinking through Christ, who gives me strength."

She repeated this over and over again. She was going to take it slowly, one step at a time. It was also about time for her to move on and forget about Keith. Their relationship had been on and off for a while now. It was a toxic relationship. They drank a lot when they were together. He was the main reason why she had not been reading her Bible, going to church, or praying lately. He was not into all these things, he said. She should have heeded her parents' warnings about him. But she wanted her independence from them and her former church. The whole thing was all too claustrophobic and predictable. She had needed a change and Keith was part of that change. But it had all been a mistake. She could see it so clearly since she came to London. The change of environment was so beneficial. She had clarity that she never had before; especially after their last conversation.

"Keith, I've been thinking about us."

"Us?"

He pretended as if he did not know what she was talking about. This time, she had no intention of letting him off the hook so easily.

"Yes, us."

"Oh, okay. That sounds serious."

"Because I am serious, Keith."

"But we have all the time in the world. We have so much to do."

"I don't, Keith."

"Okay, so what do you want?"

"I want something more."

Keith was not on the same wavelength and it was so obvious. At the time, she did not see it. But now, with hindsight, it was all so clear. She decided to video call him on WhatsApp.

"Hey, Keith."

"Hi, Divine. How is the competition going?"

She did not have the competition in mind. That was not the reason why she was calling him. She wanted to talk to him about their relationship.

"It's going okay. We've done the first round. We're preparing for the second round of auditions."

"And who are the favourites?"

"I can't discuss that and you know it."

"Even with me? Your man?"

"I didn't call you to talk about work." He must know where this was heading.

"Not again, Divine. Are you in a bad mood?"

"I'm perfectly alright."

"You don't sound like it."

"I said I'm okay! I just need to know where we stand. We've been together for years now."

"I'm simply not ready."

"Listen, I just don't have the patience to wait anymore. It's over between you and me. I have given you plenty of opportunities to get serious in this relationship. Move on with your life and I'll move on with mine."

"But, but…"

Then, suddenly, she heard a voice in the background.

"Keith, honey, come to bed."

"Who are you talking to?"

"Sorry, Divine. Got to go."

Divine could not believe it. He was actually in bed with another woman. It was good that she had put an end to their relationship. 'Thank you, Lord,' she said in her heart. She had no time for timewasters! It was like a load had been lifted from her shoulders.

Chapter XVII | The Second Round of Auditions

Lauren was looking at Nick absent-mindedly and, as usual, he was bragging. She had stopped listening to him a while ago. She was pensive and withdrawn, tired after her fitness session. She decided she would let them do the talking.

"You know my choir won the competition years ago. And thanks to that, I have been performing on TV all around the country and even internationally. I have been invited to the States, Australia, and Japan."

Divine had never even heard of him prior to the competition. But she was given a brief on all the panellists back in the States when she agreed to take up the job.

"Yeah." She caught herself almost yawning.

Lauren had heard it many times over the last few weeks during the competition preparations. He was trying to impress the pretty singer. She found him alright, but his character was a 'work in progress' as she liked to put it.

"I was also interviewed by BBC Radio, went on talk shows, and may be in line for an MBE. Why not?" he continued, trying to blow his own trumpet.

"Oh, really?" Lauren asked, knowing full well it was far-fetched.

She knew of his reputation in the music industry; it was mostly about making appearances rather than being the main man of the show. She almost felt sorry for him. Then Sean arrived. The dynamics of the group changed immediately. The tension was almost palpable. Nick could not stand the Irishman. He obviously felt threatened by Sean, who was the relaxed, funny, friendly type. In addition, he was a lot more talented than Nick was. He did not have to prove anything to anyone or show off. He was a natural.

"Where have you been? Down to the pub again?" Nick asked sarcastically.

He always liked to throw in some bad Irish jokes. Sean found it annoying at times, but just ignored him.

"Hi, ladies, how are we doing today?"

"Fine thanks. We're ready for the next round of auditions," replied Lauren with a big smile, making Nick cringe.

"Who's your favourite choir?" asked Nick, trying to draw her attention away from Sean.

"We're not supposed to discuss that until after the auditions," said Divine, breaking her silence.

"We can share our opinions."

"Nope! Not until after the auditions, I'm afraid," echoed Sean.

"When you think about it, why decide before hearing them? We don't want to feel like we're 'fixing' the competition, do we?"

"That's not what I'm saying. I'm just thinking that we can compare notes and share opinions."

Nick did not tell the other panellists that he had had a conversation with the organisers. They had a pretty clear idea of the type of choir they were looking for. They had approached Nick and asked him to try to convince the others, but he was not so sure to be able to do so now. It was a far cry from what Roger had said. They did not want a choir that would go off the beaten track or off-script. They wanted an ensemble that could sing a good old hymn with a touch of modernism, but certainly not contemporary.

What was in it for him? A lot of perks, incentives, and even TV programmes were in the pipeline if he succeeded. He had so much to lose if he could not sway the group. He was trying to seduce Lauren, but she was not falling for it. In fact, she seemed more drawn to Sean by the looks of things. Divine could not be easily manipulated and Sean, well, he was unmanageable.

"Wait till after the auditions, partner," Sean said sternly.

Nick had no choice but to drop it. He would try again later.

But he had to let the organisers know what the panellists were up to. He contacted them for an urgent meeting with his colleagues on the panel. He knew that they would not be pleased. The organiser's representatives consisted of Alex Lynch and Sally Chapman, both MBN Senior Executives; Simon Miller, MBN Art & Music Director; and Mark Pearson, MBN Press & Media Director. They turned up just as the panel was deciding who was going to take part in the last rounds of auditions. There was a little tug of war between the two groups.

"Let's be clear here; we call the shots and you follow suit," said Sally impatiently.

"Oh no! We were called upon as panellists to give our honest and informed decision, not to be puppets in your hands," responded Sean. "We owe it to all these talented contestants."

"We need to be professional and objective in our approach," agreed Divine. "What you're asking for is unethical and if this gets out…"

"Nothing will get out of this room," said Mark Pearson, "or we'll sue you for breach of contract and confidentiality. Listen, you have to realise that we've invested a monumental amount of money in this. You must go along with the script here."

"Well, you'll have to count me out," Sean said.

"And me too," echoed Divine. "I can't do it."

Lauren was cautious. She knew that they were dealing with some of the most powerful people in the entertainment industry. They had the power to make or break someone's career.

"You also have to understand that we may lose credibility if we choose undeserving winners who do not appeal to the public and the audience. This may even cause a media frenzy. People may ask questions and challenge our decision. We can't just pick a winner without justification. We have to agree to a set of criteria," Sean insisted.

"But that's what's it's all about. We want you, the panel, to agree to our criteria." Simon was doing his best to try to convince them.

"No matter what, you'll have to let us decide," said Sean adamantly. "Now, you guys should go and let us do our job."

They all looked at each other. They had no choice and had to get going. They were already behind schedule. The executives marched out of the room furious that things were not going according to plan.

***

Keisha was in her room, trying to pull herself together. Zack had been a little distant recently and it was hard for her to cope. Linda seemed to be the centre of his attention. The stunning Brazilian also appeared to be around him a lot. Keisha was having a tough time dealing with it, but she could not blame him. She was the one who asked him to slow down and give her time. Tanya had gone gallivanting with her friends somewhere in the hotel. It gave Keisha some breathing space as the girl had been asking her a lot of questions that she was having a difficult time answering. She took a while to pray for grace, strength, and peace.

Afterwards, she found her composure again and went down with the rest of the choir for the next round of auditions. They were going to sing a re-arranged version of *Oh Happy Day*. Zack and the choir had spent a lot of time working on it and were hoping that it was going to be their ticket to the final stage.

"When are we singing?" Keisha asked Agnieszka.

"You guys are near the beginning, if I recall correctly."

"Oh, that's good. Then we won't have to wait around. It saves us from getting stressed and suffering from stage fright."

The Abundant Life choir came together for a time of prayer. They were praying for the grace to sing well and for the favour of God. They needed to stay focused. Jay and the choir sang exceptionally well at the second audition. They thought that there were two or three other choirs that also did well. They believed that they should be among those going through.

***

The panel was deliberating. Again, they had about an hour to decide and there was a heated argument between the panellists. Nick wanted the choir from Berkshire to be among the finalists.

"There was nothing special about the way they sang. They're not better than the choir from Wales, for instance – they were impressive, to say the least," said Sean, annoyed.

"I was wowed by the London choir. What's their name again? Oh yes, the Abundant Life choir I think they are called," Lauren stated.

"Me too! I agree, they should go straight through along with the choir from Wales," said Divine.

"That's correct; their choreography was out of this world," added Lauren.

"So, we agree that the choirs from Wales and London should be selected, right?" Sean asked.

"Okay, that's fair enough. But now let's decide who should be the third choir to get their ticket to the final round," Nick responded.

He was very agitated as he was having a hard time trying to convince the other panellists to agree with his and the organisers' choice.

"I think the Berkshire choir is a good choice to act as a counterbalance. The other two choirs are contemporary. The Berkshire choir has a more traditional feel to their singing. My argument is that it will keep the balance."

"But then the choir from Northern Ireland was just as good if you're looking for traditional," remarked Sean.

"I don't agree with you. And I hope you're not biased because they are from Northern Ireland…"

"I beg your pardon. I'm not like that at all. It has nothing to do with that. I just want us to do right by these guys; we owe it to them. They've worked hard," an offended Sean protested.

"What is it with you? Why are you so determined for this choir to go through? There's no justification for it!" Divine intervened.

"I think they harmonised very well and brought something special," argued Nick.

"I have to agree with Nick. I think they blended their voices well, and you could feel the peace and harmony in their song. It worked well for them, I must say," stated Lauren, siding with Nick.

"That's nonsense!" Sean interjected.

"You're being disrespectful to the lady," Nick told him, trying to cause trouble between them.

"I'm just voicing my strong opinion, that's all."

"That's a bit too strong, isn't it?" Nick queried.

"Anyway, I don't agree. I'm not sure whether we were listening to the same choirs. The choir from Belfast had something much more special going on than the Berkshire choir, and we all know it!"

The argument between the two men went on for a while, with neither one willing to give in. Divine started praying silently: 'Please, dear Lord, help us.'

"Well, guys, the rule states that if there was a tie, we could pull the ace card, which counts as double. However, we only have one ace card and no more," stated Lauren.

"Oh yes, I completely forgot about that," said Divine, relieved. God had answered her plea.

Divine was to announce the shortlisted choirs. They were all present in one of the MBN auditoriums.

"The time has now come to announce the three choirs that have been chosen for the final. Let me tell you, it was not easy! We argued and debated on and on. We almost fell out. We even ended up punching each other in the face (laughs). I'm joking. I did have to pray at one stage, but fortunately, God answered my prayer. We, the panellists, have finally come to an agreement. The choirs that are going through to the final deserve to be there. Without much further ado, the finalists are the Berkshire choir, London's Abundant Life choir, and the Welsh choir."

The three choirs and their fans were overjoyed. This was such an achievement already!

"But wait, that's not all," continued Divine. "Lauren over to you."

"Well, we have a little surprise for you all. Some of my colleagues and I thought that there was a choir that also deserved another chance. We didn't want to see them go just yet. They showed astounding musical skills and there was an amazing bond between the singers. They have a great presence. So, we thought that it was only fair to them. Our first ever wildcard in the history of the competition is the Belfast choir."

The Belfast choir had surprise written all over their faces. They had not expected this at all and were ecstatic. They had made the cut. What a delight it was, especially as they had come all the way from Northern Ireland. Everyone was happy, celebrating their qualification to the grand finale.

Nick was wondering how he could convince Lauren to side with him for the final. He had to work on her before the time came, so he invited her for dinner straight after the announcement.

"There's a nice three-star Michelin restaurant not far from the MBN building. Why don't we go there this evening?"

"That would be very nice. I would love that!" Lauren was a big fan of gourmet cuisine, a fact that she had mentioned to Nick.

"Chef Marco Risoli has made a name for himself in the last five years. His restaurant serves his signature dish, 'Linguine alle Vongole', which is linguine pasta with clams in a white wine and garlic sauce. It's mouth-watering and exquisite, an experience of its own that you will never forget, I promise."

He was trying to seduce her and, if not, to win her over. That way, he could manipulate her more easily for the competition if necessary. Sean and Divine had proven tough and had shown that they were not easily swayed. He had to find a way to keep Lauren under his control. He was planning on getting her drunk or even spiking her drink. Who knows what might happen? But Nick was in for an unexpected surprise.

Lauren, on the other hand, was not deceived. She could see right through him. She decided to play along and enjoy the moment, the food, and the wine, but that was about it. She would then play a fast one on him and disappear when it was convenient for her. She laughed in her heart. What a fool!

***

Later at the restaurant, Nick asked Lauren, "Which choir do you most like?"

Lauren decided that she was going to pretend as if the wine had gone to her head and loosened her tongue. After all, he was her host. She did not want to disappoint him. She told him what he wanted to hear.

"I agree with you. I think the Berkshire choir is dope."

"Really?"

He was super happy. His job was not going to be so hard after all.

"Yes, I think I'm going to vote for them."

"I'm glad that you're on my side."

He did not realise that she was playing him. He really was gullible, she laughed to herself. Deception was the name of the game. She suspected him of working with the organisers anyway. That would teach him to try to use her. It had just cost him an expensive Italian dinner with wine. He even attempted to come on to her.

"Maybe you and I can have a little something going?" he mustered the courage to ask, but only when he was a little drunk.

Lauren herself was a little tipsy, but not enough to fall for him. He was simply not her type.

"Nick, we're just having a nice time. You know, this lovely restaurant, the ravishing food, the exquisite wine. Nothing more, nothing less."

"Come on. Things could work between us."

"I don't think so. We're having fun here. Let's not spoil things."

"Why don't you give me a chance?"

"Because I already have someone in my life."

This was a half-truth. She was interested in someone else, but she did not know whether the feeling was mutual. It was still at an early stage.

"I'm not good enough for you. Is that what you're saying?" he said with a little aggression.

"Look, don't turn weird on me. I'm just being upfront with you."

"Alright. I think we can go now."

He was a little disappointed, but at least he had partly got what he wanted – she would vote for the Berkshire choir. Or so he thought.

Chapter XVIII | Young David Chosen to be King

"How's is it going with Keisha?" Cynthia was asking her son. She could sense that something was not quite right between them.

"Nothing is going on, Mum."

"How come? The chemistry between you two is so great. Everyone can see it."

"Well, Keisha doesn't see it that way."

"Maybe there are too many people around, don't you think?"

"I don't know… I don't understand women sometimes."

"From talking to her, I can see that she is a very private person. She likes to keep her stuff to herself."

"And that's the reason why she is still alone after all these years."

"You have to be patient with her. Don't be too hard on her."

"That's what I'm trying to do. Give her space."

"Don't be too distant though. Don't act as if you're punishing her or trying to get back at her or something."

"I'm not, but it's hard on me as well, you know."

"I know, but you have to be sensitive and not seem rude or obnoxious about it. Sometimes you have to take risks for the one you love."

"I took a risk by telling her. I could be hurt too, you know."

"Yes, but you were courageous enough to go for it; now just be patient. She'll realise that you're alright. Whatever went on years ago is in the past."

"Well, I need to focus on now and get ready for tomorrow."

Clive came over to them.

"How are you doing, Son?"

"I'm alright."

"How are the preparations for tomorrow going?"

"We just had a meeting and prayer session. We're optimistic and everyone is in high spirits following our selection. From twenty down to three, that's quite an achievement!"

"We're so proud of you."

"Thank you so much for introducing us to Jay, Dad. He's been a godsend. He is so creative and talented. And to use his musical gift for the Lord is a real blessing. He could easily crossover to secular music. What made him leave the ministry he was working for, Dad?"

"I'm not quite sure. He had some kind of issue with them and he was asked to leave. It was at a time when we went away to Jamaica for a few months after retiring from ministry. He was let go by the time we came back. But I always made sure I kept in touch with him, you know. No matter what, we have to show love. We have to meet people where they're at. And sometimes it's so difficult for the younger generation to cope with the demands of our society. He seemed to be a serious and well-balanced young man. Although, sometimes I can't help but feel that he needs to get closer to the Lord. He is very passionate about music, but not half as passionate about the Lord."

"You could help him with that, sort of like a mentor."

"I don't know about that; he has to want it. Anyway, I'll try to talk to him about it after the competition. Right now would be the wrong time for that."

"You're probably right."

"When are you and Mum planning to go back to Jamaica?"

"I'm not sure, Son. It might be next year or the year after. We're looking to make arrangements to spend winters there, as the climate is milder. We will be sharing our time between Jamaica and the United Kingdom."

"Oh, I see. You know, every time I think of Jamaica, I think of the movie Cool Runnings."

"Ha ha." His father laughed out loud.

"That scene where Sanka is singing and a passer-by comes and says 'I'll pay you a dollar to shut up!' always cracks me up!"

"Or when Derice explains it's kind of like a winter sport. And Sanka answers 'you mean winter as in… ICE?'" Cynthia said in stitches.

"I liked the scene where Yul Brynner did his speech and showed Sanka a photo with a palace on it. He tells Sanka that he wants to live in the palace. Sanka laughs and replies that it's Buckingham Palace in the photo. He says: 'If you're planning on living there, you're gonna have to marry the Queen!' Yul Brenner's face is a classic. A brilliant sports comedy movie," Clive said.

"For me, the most hilarious scene has to be when Derice asks 'Sanka, ya dead?' 'Ya, Man!' That movie is legendary; a comedy classic. I've watched it countless times. Whenever I mention I have some Jamaican blood, people remind me of that film. And for a long time, I would play it at Uni. But it's been years since I've watched it."

"But darling, don't forget we also have to visit Cameroon," Cynthia reminded Clive.

"Oh yes, my love. I forgot about that."

"I'll make sure I remind you, my darling husband," she smiled with a wry smile.

Then she turned to her son.

"When you think of Cameroon, what do you think of, Son?"

"Roger Milla and the 1992 match against England at the World Cup in Italy. That was priceless, Mum."

"Yes!!! It was historical," she replied, so proud of her native country."

"I still can't get over him dancing by the corner flag each time he scored!"

Zack and his twin were always taught about both Jamaica and Cameroon. They both identified as British African West Indian. Although Zack was more in touch with the African and West Indian part of his heritage than his brother.

"Alright, I better go and get some rest before tomorrow. Night, Mum. Night, Dad."

"Good night, Son."

***

Roger knew that it was the last night before the end of the music contest. He had devised a plan to trap Jay in his net and invited him to the bar in the hotel. He used the excuse that it was for a chat for old time's sake. He knew that Jay was on his guard after what happened years ago.

"Hey, Roger," Jay greeted him from behind.

"Oh, hi, Jay. You took me by surprise."

"You wanted to talk to me."

"Yes."

"What about?"

"Well, about what happened at Living Waters Ministries…"

"That's in the past."

"But we need to address the issue."

"I don't want to talk about it."

"You can't just ignore what happened, Jay."

"I am and I have."

"Really?"

"Look, it was an accident…"

"Oh, and you really believe that?"

"It was wrong and you know it. You basically tried to take advantage and groom me."

Jay was starting to regret accepting Roger's invitation. It was a bad idea. He should have simply said no, but he knew that Roger could also prove stubborn when he wanted something.

"We can't help it."

"Speak for yourself!"

"You're just a pretender. Pretending as if nothing happened."

"If you continue talking about this, I'm going to leave. I don't want anything to do with any of that."

"Alright, alright. What do you want to drink?"

"I don't really want to drink tonight. I want to be nice and fresh tomorrow."

"You promised that you were coming down for a drink for old time's sake. It's on me."

"Okay, just one and then I'm off as I want an early night."

Roger went to get him a beer and returned. As they were talking, Julie turned up out of nowhere. She had been wanting to know a bit more about them. She knew that it was now or never.

"Hello, lads, how are we keeping?"

"We're fine and you?"

"I'm okay, Roger. Can't complain really."

"What would you like to drink?"

"Any non-alcoholic beer they've got, please."

"Okay, I'll get it."

Roger got more drinks for the three of them.

"You didn't have to get one for me, you know. I told you I will be leaving soon."

"Well, we haven't finished our conversation."

"There's nothing to add," replied Jay quickly.

"What's this about?" Julie asked. But again, Jay refused to share what Roger was on about.

"It's like this, either we talk about it now or later. It's up to you."

Roger knew he was pushing it, but he was trying to emotionally blackmail Jay with the 'talk to me later or our secret is out right in front of Miss Big Mouth' strategy.

Unfortunately for Jay, Julie was not going anywhere. She decided to stay put and see what would happen. Who knows how the drama would unfold? The conversation revolved around the music contest and what had transpired so far. Jay and Julie were trying their best to get Roger to say who the panellist's favourite choir was to win, but he was emphatic that he had no idea. He was extremely cautious after what had happened at the first audition.

After several pints of beer, Julie could see that the two guys were drunk. She was tired. She also noticed that Roger was far too affectionate towards Jay. There had most likely been something going on between them in the past. This was certainly the reason why Jay was reluctant to talk about it and acting so strange around Roger. She knew that with the two of them being drunk, she could easily expose them. This was her golden opportunity to get rid of Jay and maybe take his spot as the lead singer for the final stage of the competition.

"Come on, you guys need to go to bed. What number is your room, Jay?"

Jay was that inebriated that he handed his key card over to her.

She took them both to Jay's room and waited until they were in bed. She then took his key card and disappeared into her own room, determined to wake up very early the next morning. She was sure that by then there would be enough proof to incriminate Jay. She could not wait; she was too excited to sleep.

***

At 6 a.m., Zack was awoken by his phone ringing. It was Julie calling him. He wondered what the issue was this time. She could be a pain in the neck. But as a leader, he had to lead by example and be patient.

"Hi, Julie, what's the matter?" Zack asked, trying to use a friendly tone.

"Can you come to room 184? It's on the first floor. There's a situation."

"What's the problem?"

"I think you need to come straight away."

Zack was wondering if it was absolutely necessary for him to be there. But he knew Julie well enough to know that she would not give up easily. The sooner he got there, the better. Then, hopefully, he could still get back to bed and catch some more sleep. He went down one floor and found Julie standing outside the door of the room. She promptly opened the door to let him in.

"Look at what's going on."

"Is this your…"

But before he could finish, he saw Jay and Roger in bed together. He could also see some cannabis paraphernalia on the floor. Julie was delighted with herself.

"What are you two doing here?" asked Jay, totally confused when he opened his eyes. "I don't recall inviting you into my room."

Just then, Roger woke up, and realising what had happened, took one of the sheets, grabbed his clothes and shoes, and ran off to his room. He could not let the organisers know that he had anything to do with the contestants. He could lose his job.

Zack was furious. Julie was putting them on the spot and it was the wrong time for this to be happening.

"I thought you might want to know that your lead singer has a few skeletons in his closet."

"Julie, this is so mean of you. Did you have to go to these lengths?"

"I'm just making sure that our lead singer has the same values as ours. But he obviously hasn't."

"You're vile, Julie," said Jay, disgusted.

"Never mind, this is not about me. It's about you. What are you going to do about it, Zack?"

"You need to get out of my room. I never invited you in the first place. And how did you get in here anyway?" he asked, looking at her suspiciously.

"You gave me your key card, remember?"

"I don't remember a thing. Get out of my room now!"

"But…"

"You need to go, Julie," said Zack. "I need to talk to Jay."

Julie was sure that this was the last they would hear of him. Good, that was one of her issues sorted! It was not that difficult, was it? She was certain that they would be desperate for a replacement, and who could this be other than herself? She had a very lofty opinion of herself. She forgave them for not choosing her in the first place, although she thought it disdainful. Now, they would see how important she was for the choir, after all. She had to tell Olivia, Uche, and Mike the good news. She was sure they were going to share her joy.

***

Samuel was now an old man. He was known around Israel as the prophet of God.

Now the Lord said to him, "How long will you mourn for Saul, since I have rejected him as king over Israel? Fill your horn with oil and be on your way. I am sending you to Jesse of Bethlehem. I have chosen one of his sons to be king."

"How can I go? If Saul hears about it, he will kill me."

"Take a heifer and say, 'I have come to sacrifice to the Lord.' Invite Jesse to the sacrifice, and I will show you what to do. You are to anoint for me the one I indicate."

Samuel did what the Lord said. When he arrived at Bethlehem, the elders of the town trembled when they met him. They asked, "Do you come in peace?"

"Yes, in peace; I have come to sacrifice to the Lord."

He consecrated Jesse and his sons and invited them to the sacrifice.

When Samuel saw Eliab, he thought, 'Surely the Lord's anointed stands here before the Lord.' But the Lord said to Samuel, "Do not consider his appearance or his height, for I have rejected him. The Lord does not look at the things people look at. People look at the outward appearance, but the Lord looks at the heart."

Then, Jesse called Abinadab and had him pass in front of Samuel. But Samuel said, "The Lord has not chosen this one either."

Jesse then had Shammah pass by, but Samuel said, "Nor has the Lord chosen this one."

Jesse had seven of his sons pass before Samuel, but Samuel said to him, "The Lord has not chosen these."

So, he asked Jesse, "Are these all the sons you have?"

"There is still the youngest," Jesse answered. "He is tending the sheep."

"Send for him, we will not sit down until he arrives."

"Tee, wake up. Wake up, Tee." Keisha was calling her daughter, shouting to get her to wake up.

"Oh no, Mum. You woke me up at the wrong time!"

"What do you mean?"

"David was about to be anointed the king! I didn't get to finish the most important part of the dream, Mum. That's so annoying! I wish I could go back to my dream!"

"Well, too bad. You need to go and have your shower and then meet us downstairs once you're ready. I'll be with Clive and Cynthia in the breakfast room next to the big restaurant."

"Alright, Mum."

"Be fast about it. We have a prayer session before the final."

Keisha decided to call Pastor Kweku's wife Aunty Fifi for a woman to woman, heart to heart conversation. She needed the sound advice of a mature and wise woman like her.

"Hi, Keisha, how are you doing?"

"I'm fine. I'm busy with the competition, as you can imagine."

"I trust God that you guys will do great."

"Please, God."

"How can I help you, Keisha?"

"I just need some advice."

"Okay, go on."

"It's about Zack. He's shared his feelings towards me. He is interested in a solid relationship between the two of us."

"How do you feel about that?"

"That's why I need your help."

"Well, do you love him?"

"I have feelings for him that I haven't had for anyone in a long time."

"That's a good start. Have you prayed about it?"

"Yes, I have. But I'm so confused. I think I'm too afraid to be hurt again."

"Okay, let's pray about it. Pray that God will give you peace and that He will remove the fear and confusion. Let Him show you if he is the right man for you."

Keisha felt that he might be the one. But she was looking for more confirmation. Time would tell.

Chapter XIX | Second Chance

"**My**, my, you have some explaining to do, young man."

"Well, I'm sorry, Zack. I'm so sorry."

"Tell me. What happened?"

"Julie, Roger, and I went out last night. We had too much to drink, I guess."

"And how did you two end up in your hotel room?"

"I'm not sure. All I remember is that we were drinking and chatting away. Next thing I know, I saw you and Julie standing there."

"How did you find yourself in bed with Roger?"

"As I said, I don't know."

"Did you have a relationship with Roger?"

"Yes, in the past."

"Really?"

"Yes, but nothing happened this time."

"How do you know?"

"I was drunk, not unconscious."

"Right, you know our values and standards."

"I'm really sorry, Zack."

"You are a real disappointment. I vouched for you."

"I know I shouldn't have been drinking. I really apologise for that."

"Your future in the choir is now in doubt."

"Oh, please…"

"I worked really hard to get you into the choir, but you let me down. You let us all down."

"It's not what you think; let me explain…"

"It's too late for that," said Zack, very annoyed. "You should have thought about the consequences before you went boozing. Right, I need to go. I'll get back to you in a short while."

Jay felt sorry and bad. He was trying not to cry. He was disappointed and angry at himself. He had let himself down. It was all a terrible mistake. He had to think fast. What could he do?

'Please Lord, help me, please. I promise I will serve you for the rest of my life,' he prayed silently. *If only I could talk to someone*, he thought.

After taking his shower, he went downstairs and bumped into Keisha.

"Hi, Jay."

"Hi, Keisha. Do you have a moment?"

"Yes, what's up?"

"I need to talk to you."

"Alright, I'm going for breakfast."

"Do you mind if I join you?"

"No, of course not."

They found a table at the restaurant and ordered an English breakfast for two. Jay poured his heart out to Keisha as he was well aware that she and Zack were close. There was a rumour swirling around that something was going on between the two of them. He was hoping that she could intervene and get Zack to reverse his decision.

"But that was a bit dumb, Jay. Why would you go on a drinking spree the night before the final?"

"I know, I shouldn't have. But Roger and Julie got me into it."

"How come Zack got to know?"

"Julie."

"Why am I not surprised?"

"I think it was a setup. That Julie was behind it all, with some help from Roger."

"Right, but you haven't told me what actually happened. It must have been something serious for Zack to even consider removing you from the choir."

"Julie had my key card and brought Zack to my room. Unfortunately, I was in bed with Roger. He had dropped some cannabis on the floor. It looked like we had been smoking marijuana."

"What? You're joking, right?"

"We didn't do anything," he said quickly. "Yes, I confess that in the past, we had something going on. I was barely eighteen years old. He took advantage of me. I was so young, going through an identity crisis. He tried to groom me. As for the cannabis, I had none of it. It must have fallen out of Roger's pocket."

"My Lord, did you tell anyone about the grooming and stuff?"

"I didn't, but someone told my former church about us. It was one of the most traumatic experiences that I've ever gone through. The church I was attending didn't give me the chance to explain. They had been given false information. They excommunicated me. However, I managed to put all this behind me. This music competition was my opportunity to get back on track. And now this! I feel that history is repeating itself. Zack did not give me the chance to defend myself either. It's so unfair! I stand to lose so much in this. I can't stand by and watch this opportunity vanish just like that, Keisha."

"Calm down! There's got to be a way out of this."

"Can you talk to Zack for me?"

"I'll try. One thing that can get you out of this predicament is if Roger confirms what you're saying."

"I can call him and put him on speakerphone."

"Alright, let's call him."

"Actually, he is over there. Hey, Roger!"

He approached their table and stood opposite Keisha. He looked slightly startled.

"Hi, Jay, how can I help you?"

"I'm trying to convince Keisha that nothing went on between you and me."

"Absolutely. Julie managed to take us to Jay's room. I must confess that I encouraged him to have too much to drink, but she didn't do much to stop us. Quite the contrary, it looks like she was encouraging us, now that

I think of it. She then directed us to his bedroom. What her motive was, I really don't know."

Jay knew that the last thing Roger probably wanted was a scandal. He would already be in trouble for mixing with a contestant, and Jay wondered if his job was on the line.

"Yeah, it's true. She could have taken you to your room instead of mine if she really wanted to help," added Jay.

"It sounds to me like she ambushed you. Alright, thanks for your input, Roger. That was very helpful. We'll see you later."

"See you guys," he said, waving goodbye.

"It seems to me that they both wanted you drunk. He was busy buying you all these drinks but it eventually got the best of him too."

"Do you think you can talk to Zack for me now that Roger confirmed what happened?"

"I'll see what I can do. I can't promise anything."

"Thanks, Keisha, I owe you one."

"And a big one at that."

She called Zack for a little chat. They agreed to meet at the park outside the hotel. He was curious to hear what she had to say.

Once they were both seated on a bench, Keisha said, "It's about Jay."

"What about him?" He was a bit disappointed. He had hoped that she was going to say that she had changed her mind, and that she was willing to give them a try.

"Well, he opened up to me this morning."

"So, you're aware of what happened last night?"

"Yes, but it's not what you think, Zack."

"They were caught in a very compromising situation."

"Let me explain what actually happened."

She proceeded to repeat all that Jay and Roger had told her earlier on.

"I suppose I should have listened to the young lad before jumping to conclusions. The build-up to the final and the stress must have clouded my judgment."

"It would be a shame for him to be robbed of this opportunity so close to the final. It wouldn't be right."

"I agree it would be an injustice. However, I have a conference call scheduled with Pastor Martin and Pastor Kweku. So, it's not entirely up to me. I also have to report it to the Board of Trustees because our internal rules have been breached. Thanks for letting me know what actually transpired. I will pass it on to them. Then, they'll have to decide what the next step is. But I have to speak to Jay and Roger so that I have a first-hand account of what took place."

An hour later, Zack was on a Skype call with Pastor Martin – who had interrupted his sabbatical – and Pastor Kweku.

"I'm sorry to disturb you on your break, Pastor," said Zack.

"No worries, you just had to follow our ministry's policies. Besides, if there's a big decision to be taken involving the ministry, I sure want to be part of it. Whatever we decide will have an impact, not just on Jay, but on others, too. We have to be clear about the rationale behind our decision."

"What really happened?" Pastor Kweku asked.

"It's all a misunderstanding. I spoke to the two guys involved. The truth is they did go binge drinking. Roger and Julie pushed Jay to get drunk. But Julie was the one who instigated most of the events of last night. She led them both to Jay's room, probably hoping that they would sleep together. She took Jay's key card and then proceeded to call me and lead me to the room. You could tell she wanted them to be caught in a compromising position. She never did anything to stop any of this."

"That's not right. If she had played her role as a Christian, things would not have gone this far," Pastor Martin pondered.

"Now, it's true he did fall by drinking alcohol while representing the ministry," Zack continued, "and we need to hold him accountable for that."

"He that is without sin, first cast a stone, John 8:7," quoted Pastor Martin. "It reminds me of the powerful sermon Pastor Kweku preached in church a while ago."

"That's right. But we don't want to be seen to be condoning sin either; otherwise, we will be opening up pandora's box here."

"That's a good call," commented Pastor Martin.

"We can suggest that he stays in the choir on the condition that he attends our discipleship classes and counselling sessions with Mrs Kalu. In addition, he should be mentored; I think you would be a good fit for that, Zack."

"That's a good suggestion, Pastor Kweku. That way, he is not only being held accountable but also supervised. We will also need a progress report every three months," added Pastor Martin.

"I have some concerns about Julie," added Zack. "She's proving far too toxic for the choir. I mean, look at the role she played. She could have been her brother's keeper, but instead…"

"I suggest we suspend her for a period of one year. She was literally Jay's stumbling block. It could have turned ugly and led to something sinister like sexual assault. That was some seriously reckless behaviour on her part. She needs some time off to rethink her ways. She also needs to attend the discipleship classes for the second time. If, after a year, her behaviour does not improve, then we will have to let her go from the choir for good."

"Right, Pastor Martin. What are we going to do regarding this Roger guy? I understand that he attempted to groom Jay in the past. And now, he tried to sneak back into his life. He has the behaviour of a sexual predator. I'm not comfortable seeing him around Jay."

"I think we should come down strong on him to get him off Jay's back," Pastor Kweku interjected. "He is a bad influence and could jeopardise this young man's future. We, as a ministry, need to nurture and help him grow and mature into a minister of praise and worship. We could raise a complaint to the organisers."

"I have the contact details for Alex Lynch and Sally Chapman, the two senior executives."

"Contact them immediately," instructed Pastor Martin, "and try to organise a conference call."

Zack was able to contact Sally, but Alex was unavailable. A Zoom call was set up straight away.

"Hi, Sally, I believe you know Assistant Pastor Kweku, but you haven't met our Senior Pastor who went on sabbatical."

"Hello, Pastor Martin and Pastor Kweku."

"Hiya, Sally. It's a pleasure to meet you."

"Hi, Sally, I hope you're well."

"I'm fine thank you, Pastor Kweku. I hope all is well with you both. I understand that there is a situation at hand. I'm representing the organising team."

"Great," Pastor Martin answered. "We do have an issue that we really want to resolve ASAP. It's to do with a member of your team."

"Who's that?"

"We believe his name is Roger."

"Oh yes, Roger. I can't remember his surname right now; I can vaguely picture him."

"We want to raise an official complaint. He engaged in some inappropriate behaviour with a member of our choir. He got one of our young members drunk last night and got too close for comfort. This was highly unprofessional on his part."

"I do sincerely apologise if this is the case. We pride ourselves on hiring the best professionals in our field. This is the first time this has ever occurred. We will begin an internal investigation and get back to you as soon as we have an outcome, Pastor Martin."

"Thank you, Sally. We really appreciate this. God bless you."

Zack wanted to be the one to break the good news to Jay, who must have been in a state. He felt for the young man. He must have been feeling heart-wrenching stress, especially so close to the final.

"Hi, Jay, the leadership team and I have come to a decision. We have decided that you can stay on. However, there are conditions attached to it. I will send them to you later in the week. I think there's a lot going on right now and I want you to focus on the competition."

"Thank you so much for giving me a second chance. I won't blow it. That's a promise."

"I'll make sure you don't this time, mate."

Zack had other problems to take care of, namely Julie. He texted her and asked her to come to the reception. Julie was delighted. She was expecting some really good news. At long last, her time had come. Her hour of glory was near. She had not even had the time to speak to Olivia and co. Anyway, they would find out soon enough.

"Hey, Zack, you alright?"

"I'm okay. Right, let's not beat around the bush. I've called you regarding the incident that happened last night."

"Okay," she answered.

"I've just had a conference call with the leadership of the ministry. We've made a decision."

"Oh! Already?"

"Yes, we needed to act fast. I'm afraid I have some bad news. You're suspended from the choir for a period of twelve months."

"But why? What have I done?"

"It's rather what you didn't do, Julie. You played a bad role in this whole saga. You could have prevented what happened last night. But you chose to do nothing about it. You stood there and watched the whole thing unfold. You did not lift a finger to help your fellow choir member. We can't condone such behaviour."

"But there's nothing I could have done."

"We feel that it's quite the contrary. There were several options open to you. But you went for the worst. You showed reckless and irresponsible behaviour. You will also have to leave straight away."

"But…" she began to protest.

However, she very quickly realised that there was no use. She could not believe that she was out of the competition. Just like that. She felt numb.

She went up to her room in a daze. She did not say goodbye to anyone. Not that she had really wanted to. She was also furious. She was mad at herself, the choir, the church, and everyone. The worst thing was that her mother had come over to the United Kingdom and was at home anticipating her return. Julie was not in the right frame of mind to have a discussion with her. She took her belongings and went back home.

***

Her mother was waiting for her in her flat.

"Julie, we have to talk about your future marital arrangements."

"Mum, don't start."

"There are many suitable bachelors in Ghana. If you can't get a man here, I have contacts back home and can get my friends to introduce you to one."

"Thanks, but no thanks, Mum. I'm fine."

"What do you mean you're fine?!?" She continued in the Twi language. "Your biological clock is ticking."

"Mum, don't remind me of that."

"Okay, let me ask you… Do you at least have someone?"

Julie wanted to lie, but she knew her mum would demand to see the suitor immediately.

"Your silence says it all. Right, your way has not worked. Now, we'll try mine. Prepare to go back to Accra by next month!"

"Mother!"

"Don't 'mother' me! If you had listened to me, you would be married with two or three kids by now!"

Julie had to get rid of her mum as quickly as possible. She had to do something fast!

Chapter XX | Esther Becomes the Queen

"Good morning, Alex," Sally said in a posh high-pitched voice. She had rung him to brief him on the recent events.

"Morning, Sally. How are you?"

"It's been a tough morning, Alex. Sorry to bother you like this on a Sunday."

"What's wrong?"

"We landed our first ever formal complaint. And it was not pleasant at all. It was horrible."

"What happened?"

"Do you remember Roger? He is one of the assistants we hired recently."

"Yeah, I think I vaguely remember him."

"Well, the Senior Pastor of Abundant Life Ministries lodged a complaint saying he behaved like a sexual predator towards one of their guys. He got him drunk, and they ended up in bed together. They both claimed that nothing happened."

"That Roger was out of line. If this proves to be true, we need to get rid of him ASAP."

"I did ring him before calling you. He confirmed that they had gone drinking. A girl lured him into the bedroom of a choir member, or something to that effect."

"Having close contact with a contestant is sufficient grounds for dismissal. I'll take care of that while you just worry about the final and the reception afterwards."

"Actually, there's something else. Did you see the papers this morning?"

"No, not really. I've been doing some gardening, so didn't have time to read or watch TV, to be honest. Let me do a little Google search and see what comes up."

"I'll have you know that the judges' deliberations for the second auditions were taped and leaked to the London Herald."

"What?!? Not again!"

"You better believe it."

"I can see that it's all over the papers and on social media. Who's the culprit this time?"

"We don't know. We will have to investigate. It's either one of the judges or someone external."

"I suggest we investigate whether it's someone external first. If it turns out to be an inside job, we can't afford to lose any of our judges so close to the end of the competition."

"I'm sure there's some financial gain involved."

"You know what? It might be a good idea to check who entered the room before the panel members met and deliberated."

"That's a brilliant idea! Why didn't I think of that? I'll contact the facilities department or security and ask them to check the security camera."

"I'm going to call that Roger guy straight away."

"Good luck with that."

Alex tried to reach Roger several times. His calls went straight to voicemail. He had no choice but to contact Agnieszka, who then had the unpleasant job of sacking him.

***

"I'm afraid, Roger, your services are no longer required," she said dryly.

He had seen it coming, but he just decided to pretend that he was surprised.

"Why?"

"'Cause you overstepped your professional boundaries."

"I didn't do anything wrong."

"Apparently, you broke the terms of your contract. Alex has tried to get in touch with you but you've not been responding to his calls. Hence, I have been assigned to do this. You must leave immediately. You'll receive an official email from the organisers in due course."

"They have no right!"

"You can take it up with them. I have nothing to do with their decision."

"This is unfair dismissal. I will go and talk to my solicitor."

"Feel free to do whatever you wish. It's up to you. As for me, I'm just executing orders here."

Roger left, furious. They would not get away with this so easily, he would see to that. He was going to call his solicitor on Monday.

***

Meanwhile, Zack had the difficult task of announcing Julie's departure.

"We had to let Julie go due to behaviour that is contrary to the ethos and standards of our ministry. May I remind you that we must behave in such a way that we do not bring this ministry into disrepute? Remember that we represent the ministry. Any bad behaviour could have an impact on the reputation of the church. But most importantly, God is watching. Ultimately, we are accountable to Him."

"Who is going to replace Julie?" someone asked.

"Olivia, going forward, you will be joining the smaller group that Julie was part of, made up of Keisha, Roy, and Uche. Before the final auditions take place, you will need to practise the part where she sings backing vocals for Jay. I know it's a last-minute thing, but I have faith in you, Olivia. You have a great voice. You have a wide range. You're not limited, so don't limit yourself. Use your whole artillery and you will go far, alright? I know, we all know, that you will do your part justice."

He knew that he needed to boost her confidence by encouraging her.

"This choir is full of skilled and talented singers. We will never be stuck for singers. That's how much faith I have in your ability to sing. It's very important to understand that we are a team. Things do happen; it comes with the territory. We must be prepared; we always have to be ready to replace or step into someone else's shoes. We have to keep going, persevere and not give up easily, no matter what. Just like the soldiers in Christ that we are. And if anyone falls into temptation, we have to be our brother's keepers."

Zack was looking at Jay towards the end of his speech. He was shaking his head up and down in agreement, knowing that he had come close to following Julie out the door. He was so grateful how God had turned things around for him. As promised to the Lord, he would serve Him diligently for the rest of his life.

***

Tanya was totally oblivious to the drama that was unfolding involving Zack, Jay, and Julie. Her mother had decided to let her sleep in. This time, the fascinating story of Esther was the focus of her dream. The king had shamefully repudiated Queen Vashti because she had dishonoured him at the banquet. A beauty contest had been organised in search of the next queen. Young women from all over the kingdom came to take part in the contest. One such woman was a young and beautiful Jewish girl called Esther. She was an orphan and had been brought up by her uncle Mordecai. She was taken into the king's palace. Nobody knew her origins. She had to have beauty treatments for twelve months: six months with oil of myrrh, and six months with perfumes and preparations for beautifying women. Tanya could smell all the spices in her dream. She could see all these beautiful young girls. She was also mesmerised by the elegance of the palace and its surroundings. She was amazed by the opulence of the architecture.

After the twelve months of treatment, the contestants would go to King Ahasuerus according to his decree. Everyone liked Esther who found favour with all the people around her. Moreover, the king loved Esther more than all the other women. She obtained more grace and favour with the king than all the other virgins. He set the royal crown upon her head and made her queen instead of Vashti. He organised a great feast for her. Holding her hand, he announced: "May I present to you your new queen, Queen Esther."

Esther had won the contest.

Tanya suddenly woke up. She looked all around her and could see that she was still in bed in her hotel room. She believed that this dream was a sign that their choir was going to win. She was so excited! She could not wait to share the dream with her mother. But Keisha had gone to get ready, as the competition was approaching.

Tanya decided to go for breakfast. Detective Slim spotted her when she was helping herself to the buffet. He had got a pass from Linda that allowed him to come and go.

"I'm famished," he said as he stood next to her. "What are you having?"

"Continental breakfast," she said confidently, helping herself to some croissants, hot chocolate, and orange juice.

"I think I will go for the full English breakfast."

He put bacon, sausages, eggs, black pudding, baked beans, tomatoes, and mushrooms on his plate.

"Do you mind if I join you?"

"Sure," she said, as she had seen him around.

He was no stranger to her, or so she thought. She felt at ease talking to him. He seemed friendly as well. She had seen him talk to various members of the choir.

"My name is Andy. You must be Tanya."

"Yes. How do you know my name?"

"Linda told me."

"Oh, okay."

"How is school?"

"I haven't been going to school for a few months now," she said innocently.

"Why is that?"

"I don't know."

"That's strange…"

Detective Slim was casually fishing out any information he could from her and at the same time trying hard to bring up any mention of Pearl.

"Did your mum not tell you why?"

"Nope, she didn't."

"When did this all start?"

"The night we left our house in a hurry."

"What happened?"

"I don't know. Pearl had come to mind me. My mum woke me up in the middle of the night and we fled to our church. That's where we met Zack."

"Did Pearl not come with you?"

"No, I don't know where she is. I haven't seen her for months."

"So, since that night, you haven't seen Pearl?"

"No, I haven't."

"How strange."

"Yeah, Mum doesn't want to tell me anything about what happened."

"Did you ask her?"

"Several times."

"And what did she say?"

"She doesn't say anything. So, I don't really know what happened that night."

Detective Slim was wondering what Keisha was hiding. First, she stopped her daughter from going to school. Then her daughter was not even aware that the childminder was dead. All this was very strange. There had to be a plausible explanation. Detective Slim saw Keisha entering the restaurant before Tanya did.

"I'd better get going, Tanya," Detective Slim said hurriedly. "I'll talk to you later."

He gulped the rest of his food down and left before Keisha reached the table.

"Hi, Mum, where have you been?"

"It's been a very busy morning. You don't want to know."

"Here comes Divine… Hi, Divine!" Tanya said enthusiastically.

They hugged each other. Keisha could tell that they were really happy to see each other.

"Thank you so much for helping Tanya with her struggles. She's so delighted and she's much happier since she spoke with you. Thanks for caring so much and taking the time to speak to her. She's been talking about you so much. I'm glad I'm finally meeting you."

"The pleasure is mine. Tanya is a lovely girl. So beautiful inside and out. You should be proud of her."

"Thank you. God bless you, Divine."

***

Sally, Stan Hamilton (the security manager), Agnieszka, and Linda all went to the security camera room. Stan was going through the video archive to try to identify who had gone into the room before the panel members. It took some time before they could locate a female figure.

"Stop! There it is!" noticed Agnieszka, who was meticulous and had an eye for details. "That's what we're looking for."

They all saw a figure going into the room.

"Is that not Shreya Gupta, the senior receptionist?"

They all took a closer look at the video footage.

"Yes, indeed. That's her," confirmed Agnieszka.

"I want her here immediately!" Sally barked in a furious tone.

"We will have to get her replaced first because I believe she's on duty today," replied Agnieszka. "We will arrange her replacement before bringing her over here."

Shortly before the final auditions, Shreya was summoned into a meeting. She was terrified. What now?

"Hello, Shreya, do you know why you've been asked to this meeting?"

"No," she answered in a small voice.

"We are investigating some events surrounding the auditions. Is there anything you have to tell us?"

"No," she said.

But everyone could tell that she was on the defensive. She looked all flushed and out of breath. "Well, we want to show you something."

They played the videotape where she was seen entering the room.

"Can you explain what you were doing in the MBN building and in this room, instead of being in the hotel reception?" asked Sally, looking very threatening.

She was silent, unable to utter a word.

"We have every reason to believe that you recorded the meeting that took place among the panel members. This meeting was confidential, and we were only going to release snippets of it to the public."

"It's not me!" she tried to protest, but did not sound too convincing.

"But we have proof on tape that you went into the room hours before their meeting and you have no proper explanation as to what you were doing there."

"But I didn't do anything!"

"Look, if you tell us the whole story, I will show leniency. But if you persist in denying any wrongdoing, then we will prosecute if needs be."

Shreya broke down in tears. She could not take it any longer.

"I… I did go into the room and place a small recording device in there. I retrieved it once everyone was out of the room and handed it to the London Herald. I'm so sorry."

"But why did you do it?"

"It's because of some personal issues I have going on. My mother is very ill back home."

"That is no excuse, Shreya. There are other things you could have done other than betray your employers."

"I'm deeply sorry for everything. I was not thinking straight because I was under so much pressure. I know it's no excuse, though."

"Well, it's too late now. The deed has been done. You will have to prepare to hand over and leave all the hotel's belongings like your badge, key card, restaurant passes, etc."

"Please, I need this job," she pleaded desperately. "My mum's life is at stake."

"You should have thought of that before you did what you did. This decision will not be reversed, Shreya," concluded Sally.

"You only showed remorse after you were confronted, Shreya," said Agnieszka, unmoved. "You never once thought of the consequences of what you did for the competition, and even if you did think about it, that didn't stop you one bit."

"How much did they offer you?" Stan wanted to know.

"Mm, mm…" Shreya did not want to say. It was not enough to carry out the operation.

"Anyway, I hope you were paid handsomely, because you're going to need it now that you've found yourself without a job."

Linda felt bad for Shreya. She agreed that it was wrong of her to have done what she did, but there were some mitigating circumstances. She hated to think of what would become of Shreya's mother now that they had dismissed her.

Shreya was devastated. The worst had happened. What would she tell her husband? Her family back in India? She was in floods of tears and went to the toilet to recover and clean her face. She did not want anybody to see her, certainly not her colleagues. She made her escape when everyone was busy preparing for the final round.

Chapter XXI | The Final Audition

Nick was hiding in his hotel room. He was in a bad mood. He thought that after their little escapade at the restaurant, something would have happened between him and Lauren, but it was not working at all. She remained disinterested and rebutted all his attempts at seducing her. In fact, she had been so alert that he was not even able to get her drunk. She was only slightly tipsy. They ended up going back to the hotel shortly after dinner, as she had received a long-distance call. He vaguely remembered the conversation they had.

"You and I, it won't work, and you know it," she said.

"But we could try."

"I already told you. You and I are not meant for each other."

"But we can enjoy ourselves, just once."

"A one-night stand, you mean?"

"Yes, why not?"

"I'm not into that at all," she said, disgustedly. "I'll excuse you this time cause you're slightly drunk. But don't push it!"

"Oh well, no harm in trying," he mumbled to himself.

"You really think I'm cheap, don't you?"

"No, I don't. We're both adults. We could just have fun together, that's all I'm saying."

"Not a chance!"

Unfortunately for Nick, the deliberations had been published in the press that same morning. Things did not look too good for him. It got people talking. He was branded biased and an unfair cheat. There was even a call for him to be thrown off the panel. He did not know where to hide his face. On the MBN Facebook and Instagram pages, Nick's story was trending, with comments being posted from all over the United Kingdom. But the abuse coming from Northern Ireland was the worst.

"That Nick! He has the guts to show up after what he has done. What a disgrace he is! He should be chucked off the panel!"

"He doesn't deserve to be a panel member."

"To think that all he has to his name is to have won the Choir of the Year competition."

He was all alone. He only had himself to blame. He was feeling the brunt of the attack. He regretted some of the things that went on during the deliberations. It was blatantly obvious that he had favoured the Berkshire choir. But this was down to the organisers. They pressured him because they wanted their chosen choir to win. He was also furious because, in the bid to have the choir go through, he was losing credibility and getting a bad name for himself. He decided to give Mark Pearson a call. After all, it was all their fault. He blamed them for the backlash. Mark was the MBN Press & Media Director; maybe he could come up with a PR stunt to turn things around. He might even convince Mark to release a statement, just to appease the public before the final auditions. His approval rating, compared to the other panellists, was going down by the day. This would not be good for his reputation. He had hoped that through his participation in the competition more doors would open to him.

"How on earth did the videotape get leaked to the press in the first place?" he asked Mark.

"One of the receptionists got caught red-handed."

"I'm going to sue her for that!"

"You're not in the best position to do that. It looks like you were ready to pick your choice of choir, rather than the best one. As a result, the public has turned against you."

"But it's your fault. You pressured me into it. Now I'm the scapegoat. You better help me. If I go down, you all go down with me."

"What do you mean?"

"I will go to the press with the full story," he threatened.

"I will have to talk to the others before I do anything, you know that."

"You don't have much time, so you better act quickly. Or else…"

"Are you trying to blackmail us?"

"Call it what you want; I don't really care. I need to get out of this mess fast before irreparable damage is done to my reputation."

"What do you want me to do?"

"I want you to release a statement denying that anything wrong has happened, and that it is all a misunderstanding. That the tape was edited in a way that gave the wrong impression of me."

"I will have to talk to the others before we do anything."

"I'll be here waiting."

Mark went to organise a conference call with Alex, Sally, and Simon.

"I just got off the phone with Nick. He is attempting to blackmail us. The chap is basically saying that we must do everything in our power to stop the backlash, otherwise, he will go public on us and divulge everything."

"We must act urgently, otherwise we will have to deal with a total fiasco," Sally said, slightly panicked.

"We can't let this happen."

"Absolutely! We cannot risk it," Alex was adamant. "Nobody must know what transpired between us and him."

"It's just as well that the Belfast choir was chosen as the wild card, otherwise we would have been in hot water today."

"Yes, that's true. Look, we can use that as a cover-up story and explain that the Belfast choir still went through, so Nick's actions didn't have that much impact after all."

"What should we do then, in your opinion?"

"We should write a statement as he suggested and try to exonerate him," said Mark.

As he oversaw the press and media coverage, he knew how to sway public opinion.

"I will try to work something out," he said, half talking to himself.

"Let's just say that it was a misunderstanding and poor judgement on his part, or something of that nature, but that it had nothing to do with being biased or cheating. After all, the Belfast choir can still win. Other choirs have already gone home. So, not all hope is lost."

"But what shall we do about the panel members?" Sally was worried.

"Well, they just need to keep their mouths shut. The last thing they need is any more controversy."

"Okay, I will draft a statement. Keep an eye on your inbox. You can comment or edit it as you see fit. We could use this to attract more attention, you know..."

"What do you mean?"

"Well, a cocktail of scandals, rumours, allegations, and controversies can be good advertising. Who wants a boring competition? So much has been going on... The viewing figures will go through the roof."

"That's right. I hadn't seen it from that perspective, but you have a point there, Mark. You're our media guy, so you know your stuff," Alex commented. "Try to work out something that we can turn to our advantage."

After some back and forth and a multitude of emails exchanged, the organisers were able to concoct a statement, which read as follows:

> *The organisers of the MBN competition deny all allegations of wrongdoings levelled against one of the panel members. There have been some disagreements between the panel members, but this is standard practice in a competition. The comments posted on social media and the press are unfounded and factually false. The information provided is also misleading, prejudicial, and reckless in nature. We, the organisers, will address the denigrating allegations propagated by certain media outlets in due course. We will not be commenting beyond this point as we wish to give the participants the space to focus on the final leg of the competition without any further distractions.*

Once the statement was released, the tide seemed to turn in favour of Nick, with people defending him. Mention was also made of the fact that the Belfast choir was taking part in the last round, so no harm had been done. Nick was now more contented with the way things had turned out. He went downstairs to join the panel.

It was now time for the final auditions. Everyone was excitedly hurrying around. Some were waiting in a long queue to get into the auditorium. Others were trying to find the best seats. The choirs that had qualified for the final round were preparing and rehearsing. After their prayer session, the Abundant Life Ministries choir was also doing a quick rehearsal.

Linda ran into Zack, and they got talking.

"Hey, Linda, how are you?"

"It's busy. We have to get everyone seated and make sure that all the teams have organised themselves. Also, we must ensure that everyone who is not staying the night has vacated their room in time. So, it's all very hectic but I think we'll be alright. What about you and the choir?"

"Well, we're all very excited. We're delighted to have made it so far and are hoping for the best."

He found her attractive, but he was looking for something serious. He had a hunch that she just wanted some fun, and certainly nothing long-term. She was giving out vibes that she did not want to get attached to anyone and had a seductive smile on her face. He was not fooled; he had seen her flirting with Detective Slim and another guy from the panel. Just then, Keisha was turning the corner of the corridor. She immediately saw them. There was an uneasy silence when she got to them.

"I'd better go. I have so much to do," Linda uttered, extracting herself from the awkward situation.

The tension was palpable.

***

"What's going on between you two?" Keisha confronted him when they were alone.

"What do you mean?"

"You seem to be spending a lot of time with Linda. It looks like you're attracted to each other," she said, sounding very annoyed.

"We're too busy for that!"

"Everywhere I go, I meet you two."

"Really? Are you jealous?"

"No, I'm not!" she denied.

"Sounds like you are. What exactly do you want?" It was his turn to confront her.

Keisha immediately regretted not keeping her feelings in check. She had lost control, unable to hide her jealousy. What was happening to her? It was very unlike her. She kept silent, embarrassed at her little outburst.

"I don't get it. I thought you said you needed your own space. That you had a lot on your plate, and wanted to sort out one or two things. So, what are you on about?"

"It's just that…"

"What?"

"No, nothing."

"You have to decide what it is that you want, you know. I try to get close to you but you keep me at bay. I leave you alone and you complain. I don't understand you women."

Keisha knew that she was a mess. One minute she wanted him, next thing she wanted to be left alone. She remembered being envious of her friend Pam getting married. What was she thinking? She needed to make up her mind. She could not continue like this. She had to decide once and for all. Enough of this indecision! Just at that moment, someone came to call their choir.

"Abundant Life Ministries choir, get ready. You're on in about ten minutes!"

There was no more time for discussions. Keisha was left all flushed and caught in the spur of the moment. What was that about? She had behaved a little over the top.

The choir found themselves on stage. Jay nailed it with the song that he wrote. Roy surpassed all expectations with his choreography. He had chosen a 1970s theme with costumes to match. It went down really well with the panellists and the public. The song and the choreography did it. There was a long-standing ovation.

***

Nick was supposed to have made the announcement, but due to the scandal in the previous round, he had been side-lined.

Therefore, Sean was standing in front of the public. There was complete silence, as if everything stood still. Not a word. Not a movement. He had succeeded in captivating his audience. All eyes were on him.

"Hi, everyone. What's the craic? Well, if you ask me, the craic has been great! I'm so fecking enjoying myself!"

People in the audience who were familiar with these Irish expressions burst out laughing. His Irish accent was making the announcement even more interesting. He was the embodiment of Irishness. He liked barhopping in the Temple Bar. He would occasionally go to George Street for a taste of the underground scene. But he was not too keen on the illegal nightclubs and the presence of drugs everywhere. No, he liked harmless craic. He grew up in church but never took it seriously, even though his parents were church leaders. Sean had the good sense of not taking himself too seriously. This made the atmosphere light-hearted and fun wherever he went. However, he had developed a thing for gospel music. There was something about it that spoke to him more than any sermon or any of his parents' lectures. He sometimes felt sorry for them. They had tried so hard to make him a youth pastor.

"You should come to church sometime," his parents would invariably say.

"Yeah, I might one of these days," he said unconvincingly. He did not want to hurt his parents' feelings. He had no interest in answering the 'call of ministry', an expression they liked to use. They often told him that he had become lukewarm. Well, he was never too 'hot' with anything to do with the church in the first place. He considered church life to be boring and just not for him. He stopped going to church as soon as he could stand up for himself against his parents. His parents would say, "we'll keep praying for you". Keep praying, he thought ironically. He thought everything was going alright. He was just not sure who to date. Niamh, Ciara, or Robyn. And now Divine. He found her 'gas' – another colloquialism, used in Ireland, meaning entertaining. She looked exotic and interesting. Lauren had tried flirting with him, but she was too bland for his liking.

"I'd better crack on, otherwise you lot are going to give out to me," he said with a big smile, making faces.

The audience burst into laughter again. He was a real clown.

"It is my privilege to announce that the winner of the 2021 MBN Gospel Choir of the Year is... Abundant Life Ministries from London!!!"

Everyone jumped to their feet to celebrate the win. It was a joyful celebration indeed. The audience was chanting "Abundant Life."

Members of the choir were hugging each other. Everyone forgot about social distancing at this stage.

***

At the reception organised by MBN, Sean decided to connect with Divine. After all, he had nothing to lose. He was a go-getter and usually went with his gut feelings. The time was right now that the competition was over.

"Hi, Divine, are you up for a bit of craic?"

She looked a bit confused, not having heard the expression before.

"You used the same word earlier on in your speech. What does it mean?"

"Oh, it's just an Irish expression. In other words, are you ready for some fun?"

"Okay, very interesting."

"So, what's your answer?"

"I am… But I recently gave up smoking and drinking, so it is a teetotal affair," she said and laughed.

"Is there no way of corrupting you?"

"You will be the bad guy if you tried. I made this promise to God."

"Christian, are you?"

"Yes, I had fallen from grace, as they say, but recent events have caused me to have a change of heart. What about you?"

"I grew up in church. My parents were church leaders."

They had a lot in common, although her faith was certainly a lot stronger than his. But to win her over, he knew that he needed to sober up.

Chapter XXII | Home Sweet Home

Questions were swirling through Julie's mind. What should she do now? Who could she get to persuade the church leaders to reconsider her exit from the choir? Who could force them to overturn their decision? She could not get over the shame. Suddenly, she had a lightbulb moment, or so she thought.

"Good evening, Pastor Kweku."

"Hello, sister Julie."

He wondered what she had up her sleeve. She was certainly not calling to exchange pleasantries, that he was sure of. But he had learnt to be extremely diplomatic with her. He had always managed to keep out of her net, and he hoped it would stay that way.

"How are you doing these days?" he asked.

"I have not been doing so well. I'm sure you know why!" she answered aggressively.

"I do know. I understand, sister. How can I help?"

"Pastor, I need to get back into the choir."

"You know you can't. You've been suspended for a year."

"But that can't happen with all that's going on. The choir is going to receive invites for TV programmes and various events. I can't afford to miss it!"

"You have no choice."

"You could help me."

"It's too late for that. The decision was taken by the senior pastor. I had no say."

"You could have defended me."

"They had already made up their minds. You did yourself a disservice by not protecting your fellow choir member, you know."

"Don't preach to me, Pastor. You have a few skeletons in your closet yourself."

"What do you mean by that?"

"You think I don't know about your little secret?"

"What are you talking about?" he asked, pretending not to know. This conversation was turning out to be a nightmare. And he had not heard the worst of it yet.

"I know about your love child."

"I don't know what you're talking about."

"I have my ears to the ground and I know for a fact that you fathered a child a while ago."

"You've got it all wrong!"

"Never mind! As you preached in your sermon a while back, nobody is perfect. Sort me out and your little secret is safe with me."

"It's not true. I don't have a love child."

Julie was having none of it.

"You have seven days. If I don't hear anything by next week, you'll be exposed!"

***

Pastor Kweku was due to have a session with Oliver and Adam at the church. It just so happened that Michelle and Caroline were also in the church. The two boys found the sessions boring. Pastor Kweku would go on and on about the Bible, the Lord, and sin. Sometimes they almost fell asleep during his teachings. They were trying to find a way to skip the session. But they had been warned that if they did, Ben would be pressing charges against them. Then suddenly, they noticed Michelle and Caroline. As usual, Caroline could not hold her tongue.

"Are you the two guys who almost killed Pastor Ben?"

The two boys were too busy staring at them. They looked at each other. Maybe they could have some fun after all.

"We didn't want to kill him; it was just an accident," said Oliver.

They both found the girls attractive. At long last, something exciting was happening at the sessions.

"I'm Oliver and this is my friend Adam. What are your names?"

"I'm Caroline and this is my friend Michelle. What are you doing here?"

"We're waiting for Pastor Kweku."

"Oh yeah, I remember. It's for the sessions."

Oliver was staring at Michelle. He thought she was charming, and she thought he was cute.

"How about we get together after our meeting with Pastor Kweku?"

"Oh no, we will be gone by then," Caroline said.

She had no interest in either of them. But now the boys had a reason to come to church, and it had nothing to do with the gospel.

***

Keisha, meanwhile, wanted to restore some kind of normality to their life. Forensics had done their investigation, and the report had been delivered to the Criminal Police Department. It was time to go back home. She had made arrangements for the house to be deep-cleaned, as it had been lying empty for months. She found a quiet time to speak to her daughter.

"Come and sit down, I need to talk to you, Tee."

They were still at Clive and Cynthia's house, pending their return home. She had asked Divine to spend a few days with them when they moved back home. Thankfully, she agreed to join them later. Keisha believed that the presence of Divine would help fill in the vacuum left by Pearl.

"You've been asking me about Pearl."

"Yes, I miss her so much. What happened?"

"I have something to tell you," she said hesitantly.

"You're scaring me, Mum."

"We lost Pearl."

"How? When?" Shocked, she began to cry.

"I can't really go into details. But she died a few months ago."

"Why didn't you tell me?"

"I didn't want to worry you. I knew you would be very sad."

Tears were rolling down Tanya's face. Keisha was trying to console her.

"You have to stop hiding things from me. I'm not a little girl anymore. I can handle things."

"I know, Tee. But you're still my baby. And you will always be." She dried her daughter's tears.

Tanya eventually calmed down. She looked at her mum intently.

"What about my father, Mum?"

"What about him?" she replied, avoiding eye contact.

"You know exactly what I mean. It's about time you told me the truth."

Keisha was quiet for a while. She realised that she could not postpone this any longer. The time had come for her to disclose the truth. She told Tanya the story. At least, most of it. She left out the bit about her son. It was too soon and too painful. Kesha felt it was not the right time to talk about Charlie. That would be a story for another day. Tanya needed time to digest Pearl's death and her father Felix's story. Tanya had taken things better than she thought. She had matured from the overly sensitive girl she used to be.

Tanya felt sad for the loss of her dearly missed childminder. But she also felt relieved because at long last she knew a bit about her past. She knew about her background and where she came from. One day, when the time was right, she promised herself she would go looking for her father.

They said their goodbyes to the Armstrongs and knew they would all miss each other. Clive and Cynthia were so loving and friendly, and they had had some good times with them. They had got to know Zack's family very well and established a very close bond with them, but now the time was right for them to go back home.

They arrived home that evening. Tanya had missed their house and was so glad to be there. For Keisha, it was another story – she had mixed feelings about going back. She had flashbacks to the night of the murder. She remembered how they had to flee late that night. Maybe it was time to sell the house and move to another place? She liked the house, but it was now tainted with the events that happened so many months before.

***

The next morning, Tanya woke up early. Mother and daughter were so happy to spend time together, just the two of them. They went cycling around the neighbourhood that they had not seen for months. They got some delicious carrot cake from the bakery shop next door. For lunch, they cooked fried chicken, squash, and collard greens to celebrate their victory at the competition and their return home.

During the afternoon, Tanya's friends, Ana and Audrey, arrived.

"So happy to see you guys. It's been such a long time."

"How have you been, Tanya?"

"Where have you been?"

"We needed to take some time off. Mum also had to attend a gospel competition."

"Oh yes, I heard about that. Your mum's choir won, right?"

"Yes, we did," Tanya said, clapping in delight. "And, guess what?"

"What?"

"Divine is joining us for a few days."

"Who is Divine?"

"A gospel singer who has won multiple awards."

"Wow, that's amazing!"

"Yes. I can't wait for her to come."

"That's exciting!"

"Would you guys like some carrot cake?"

"Yes, please."

"And what would you like to drink?"

"We'll have some tea."

"Yes, tea, please."

Tanya had missed her classmates.

"How has school been?"

"It's been okay. Of course, it's the summer holidays now."

"Are you guys going to go away?"

"We were supposed to be going to France. But we have decided to stay put because of the COVID-19 restrictions. Papa said that it's too complicated for us to travel. So, we are going to the Lake District instead. 'Pas de Paris cet été.' No Paris this summer."

"What about you, Ana?"

"My parents decided we are going to Spain. We want to see our family and friends back home."

"Girls, I have a series of games for us to play. On the menu is an egg-and-spoon race, a sack race, some dodgeball, and water pistol hide-and-seek; that's the last game as we will all be wet and we will have to get changed. That's why I asked you to bring another set of clothes. Each time we play a game, the winner will get awarded points. The one who has the most points at the end will be the overall winner and will get a prize."

"That's brilliant!" Audrey exclaimed.

"What is the prize?"

"A Gap voucher."

"We can hide in the house, in the garden, anywhere really."

The girls were having a great time. Audrey was really enjoying herself as she was currently winning. The water pistol hide-and-seek was particularly fun and the girls were almost hysterical with laughter. Then, Tanya found something on the ground – a business card that was under a shrub in the shade. She wondered what it was doing there and thought that her mum must have inadvertently dropped it or something. She ran into the house.

"Mum, look what I found. Is it yours?"

"What is it?"

"Somebody's business card."

She took a close look at the business card. It contained somebody's name she didn't know: Mark Forsyth. It stated on the card that he was a bodyguard and close protection operative. The strange thing was that her name was handwritten on the back of the card. It had faded because of the length of time it had been exposed to the elements, but it was still legible. Why was her name on it?

She instinctively knew this was a very important piece of information. God might just be giving them a helping hand. Was this the vital clue they needed? And would it lead them to the killer? She decided to keep her thoughts to herself and refrained from saying anything in front of Tanya and her friends.

She went onto the internet, Googled his name, and came across a certain Mark Forsyth. He had spent time in jail for a contract killing and had been released a few years ago. He was also a well-known criminal, part of the underworld, and was a close associate of a drug lord. It looked like after his release he had been trying his hand at bodyguarding. What was his business card doing outside their house? She wondered how the police had missed it. She went back outside to check out the place where it was found. She remembered that her daughter had found the business card under a shrub. This explained how they had missed it and how it had been preserved so well after all these months. God was on their side. This was a remarkable and unexpected piece of evidence. However, she could not help shivering. She feared for their lives. Danger was looming. Did they do the right thing by coming back home? Was their life in any danger?

Audrey was the overall winner of the games. She was so delighted with herself as she was known to loathe losing. She had taken a while to get over that Kahoot loss months before. This was a really good afternoon for her.

***

Detectives Hunt and Slim were in Claire's office. They recognised her from her LinkedIn profile, though she looked slightly plumper. She was wearing a forced smile on her face; she did not look comfortable and avoided eye contact with them, as if she was trying to hide something.

"Sorry I didn't catch your names."

"I am Detective Hunt, and this is my colleague, Detective Slim."

"How can I help you?"

"We're investigating the murder of Keisha's childminder," said Detective Hunt.

"I don't get it. Whose murder?" she looked totally lost.

"Keisha's childminder, Perla Bautista... When was the last time you saw Keisha?" Detective Hunt asked.

At that moment, it dawned on her that Keisha was still alive after all. She had initially thought that they were coming to inform her of Keisha's demise. How stupid was she? She should have known that something was not right when she did not hear anything for months. But she had not wanted to raise any suspicions.

"Keisha is on sabbatical," she offered as an explanation, not knowing what to think, or in fact, what to say. She decided to play along and pretend as if all was normal.

"Don't you know what happened?"

"No, I don't," she said with feigned innocence.

"Pearl was murdered at Keisha's home. We think that Keisha was the actual target. We understand that she hasn't been at work. You're saying that she took some time off, right?"

"I believe she still has about a few months or so left. I'm not quite sure when she's due to return."

"We thought you might have some idea and may be able to help us with our investigation."

Claire was trying to hide her panic. She looked shocked and overwhelmed.

"No," she replied a bit too quickly.

"Did you notice anything out of the ordinary before she went away?"

"I can't think of anything right now. It was a while ago, you know..."

"Did she strike you as being in any kind of trouble? Was she afraid?"

"I wouldn't know, because Keisha is a private person. She would keep her personal life to herself. We've worked together for years, but I wouldn't describe us as being close."

"Why do you think she took a sabbatical?"

"I'm not really sure. Maybe she just wanted a break."

"But why is that? Was she stressed, or did she have issues at work?"

She just shrugged her shoulders.

"I have no idea. Anyway, she's been working for the firm for many years. So, as such, she is entitled to a sabbatical."

"Do you think she was running away from something?"

"As I said, I wouldn't know."

"From what you know of her, did she have any enemies?"

"I wouldn't have a clue. Keisha would not confide in me. Like I just said, we are not that close."

"Are there any colleagues that she is close to?"

"She was friendly with everyone. But no, she was not particularly close to anyone that I know of."

Detectives Hunt and Slim looked at each other. They were not getting anywhere with Claire.

"Well, it's time for us to take our leave. Here is my card. If you think of anything else, please give us a call."

"I sure will, goodbye."

Claire immediately made a phone call. She was in a state of panic. Her heart was beating fast.

"Mark, what have you done?"

"What's wrong?"

"You've messed up big time!"

"What have I messed up?"

"Keisha is alive."

"What? Impossible!"

"I'm telling you?"

"You're not serious! How do you know?"

"The police just visited, asking questions. You killed the wrong person!"

"How come you're only learning this now?"

"Well, because the police came looking for her."

"What are we going to do now?"

"You better finish the job we paid you for!"

Mark's business as a bodyguard had fallen on hard times due to the pandemic. He had accepted the job for extra cash. He just could not resist the temptation. He was now regretting his decision with the new turn of events.

"It will be too risky now that the police are on our trail."

"I don't care how you do it, just do it! We have very little time on our hands. Clean up your mess!"

She hung up the phone, furious. She then tried to contact Keisha, but there was no response. She left a voicemail asking her to call her back as soon as she got the message.

***

Meanwhile, back at the police station, the chief detective inspector was holding a meeting with Detectives Hunt and Slim.

"How did it go?"

"We couldn't get anything out of her. But we could not shake off the feeling that she knows something. Or rather, she's hiding something. She looked very fidgety when we were asking about Keisha."

"Yes, definitely!" added Detective Slim.

"We need a search warrant. We will also need to bring her to the station for questioning."

"It will be ready in three days; that's the best I can do."

"We better keep an eye on Keisha and Tanya. You never know, the danger might come from Keisha's workplace. By us going there, we might have inadvertently alerted the killers that we are on their trail."

"Very true. I'll put Detective Kelleher and another guy on the case. Detectives Hunt and Slim, you take care of Claire."

"Okay, boss."

Chapter XXIII | Confession Time

Xylophone sounds were coming out of Tanya's bedroom. Shouting and laughter could be heard. Occasionally, Keisha could hear some banging. Divine had come to stay with them for a few days, at her invitation. The girls were in a crazy mood. She hoped it would help Tanya cope with Pearl's death. Right now, they were having fun with a musical instrument. However, Keisha was preoccupied with Tanya's discovery the day before. She felt that they were in imminent danger. Home might not be so sweet after all. She also saw Claire's missed call and heard the voicemail. She suspected that Claire was aware that she was still alive.

What should they do? They could not go back to Zack's parents. Staying in a hotel was out of the question. Could they find refuge in the church? That would mean moving again. Besides, it was not proper accommodation. She decided to call Zack and tell him about the situation.

"Hi, Zack, how are you?"

"I'm doing great. I've been resting since we came back from the competition."

"That's great, a well-deserved rest."

"Also, we got invited to perform at different Christian conferences and gatherings."

"Really? So fast?"

"Yes, I'm as surprised as you. We will need to rehearse."

"I might not be able to make it, you know."

"And why is that?"

"Well, Tanya found a business card right outside our house that turned out to belong to an ex-criminal."

She began to explain to him what she found out online about Mark Forsyth.

"You need to be extremely cautious," he said.

"What do you suggest we do?"

"You need to lie low again."

"I was trying to avoid that, for Tanya's sake. She needs some normality in her life after the past few months."

"But not at the expense of safety."

"You're absolutely right."

"Why don't you go to the police?"

"I don't want to alarm Tanya and Divine. I didn't tell Tanya the circumstances surrounding Pearl's death and how violent it was because I didn't want to frighten her."

"Oh, I see. How are you going to explain to them that you all have to leave?"

"I'm not sure how to go about it. I might wait until I'm alone with Divine. I will explain things to her once Tanya has gone to bed."

"Alright, fair enough."

"Then we'll decide what to do next. How are your mum and dad?"

"They're doing great. Proud of us, as you would expect. They're really delighted that we won the competition. They're talking about it to everyone, everywhere they go."

"I can well imagine. I miss all of that. I miss you."

"I'm glad to hear that. I thought you were never going to say it."

"What do you mean?"

"We have to stop pretending, Keisha. I still have strong feelings for you. They haven't gone away. If anything, they're even stronger than before. I hope you're not playing the friendship card here. I have lots of friends, thank you very much. As I told you before, I'm looking for something more. I love you."

Keisha remained silent for a while. She could not pretend anymore. She could not hide her feelings. It was confession time.

"I love you too."

***

Zack was shocked. He had hoped to hear those words for so long. And now he felt like he was in a dream.

"Say that again."

He wanted to make sure he had heard correctly.

"I love you too."

He was ecstatic. He threw his fist in the air. At long last.

"We have to celebrate this."

"Okay," she said and laughed. "How?"

"Why not come over for some dinner? But first, we need to sort out this situation with Mark Forsyth."

"That's right, totally agree."

"You can talk to Divine tonight. And tomorrow it might be worth going to the police. I think you guys need to be under some kind of police protection."

"I would certainly feel safer if the police were around. But I will talk to Divine and see how it goes."

***

Keisha was having a cup of tea with Divine. She had to let her in on what was going on.

"As you know, Pearl died a few months ago. She was murdered right in this house. Tanya doesn't know."

"Wow, that's shocking."

"The thing is, we discovered a business card that belongs to a man who was in prison and now claims to be in security, just outside our home. Mark Forsyth is his name. I'm worried that he might come back for us. I'm trying to work out what to do next."

"Right, I get you."

"I don't think it's safe to stay here. There is a killer on the loose."

"I'm in London for the next two weeks. I rented a four-bedroom house in Chelsea. I intended to visit London and other places. We could go and spend some time there."

"What should we tell Tanya? She's so happy to be back home. I didn't want to have to uproot her again. And she's going to ask questions."

"I'll just say that I need some company and that I would love to have you both staying with me."

"Yeah, that could work. I mean, she loves you. I'm sure she would really love to spend a lot of time with you. All I ever hear these days is Divine this and Divine that," she said, laughing.

"We just get along so well despite the age gap."

"It's just incredible the way she took to you so quickly."

"She is like the little sister I never had."

"And you are the big sister that she never had," Keisha said, laughing again.

They made arrangements to move to Divine's place. But little did they know what lay ahead.

***

Pastor Kweku was in a state. He had tried pleading with Julie, but to no avail. She was adamant that he talk to the senior pastor about overturning the decision. She would just not accept that this was not possible. He could not reason with her. And now he was in a dilemma. He was thinking of his wife and his family. How they were going to be so hurt. But there was no way out of it. His mobile phone rang; it was Julie again.

"Pastor Kweku, I am calling to remind you that tomorrow is the deadline."

"Sister Julie, I'm pleading with you. Think of my wife and my family. Think of the damage it will do to the church, the ministry."

"What about me? Did you think about how I felt when I was kicked out of the choir? Do you know how I feel right now?"

"I'm sorry, sister Julie, and I do feel for you."

"It's too late for that, Pastor."

"Nothing will change your mind, I guess."

"Absolutely nothing."

Julie was relentless. Pastor Kweku knew that there was nothing he could say or do to make her change her mind. They ended their phone conversation. He went to his study. He had served as an assistant pastor for over ten years and stood to lose everything. The ministry he had built was going to fall apart before his very eyes. He was slumped in his favourite chair when his wife came into the room.

"Hi, honey, are you alright?"

"I'm okay."

"Are you sure? You look a bit out of sorts. Have you checked your BP?"

"I told you, I'm okay. I just have a lot on my mind at the moment."

"Do you want to talk about it?"

"No, it's fine. Don't worry about it."

"Okay, if you say so."

Pastor Kweku knew she was concerned because he usually told her everything. He guessed that she would be questioning what the problem could be since they had a strong marriage and were the model couple in the church. They were best friends, and even though their life together was not perfect, they were a happy family.

He needed to spend time alone with the Lord. He also needed to search himself. Where did he go wrong? He had gone far from the Lord. He realised that he wasn't praying as much as he used to. He would seldom open his Bible, except for sermons, and had gone so cold towards the Lord. He no longer had time for devotion. He was so afraid. Afraid of what his fellow Christians, ministers, and leaders would think of him. The thought of his wife. And his pastor. What had he done to himself? His misdeed had caught up with him. He prayed earnestly. He needed to ask God, his wife, his family, and his church for forgiveness. Once his wife left the room, he fell to his knees in repentance, sobbing. It was time to take responsibility for his actions.

***

"Pastor Martin, we need to talk."

"It sounds like confession time," he tried to joke.

But Pastor Kweku was not laughing.

"It sounds pretty serious. Let me switch off my mobile phone so that we can talk without disturbance."

"I messed up, Pastor. I don't even know where to start."

"Start at the beginning."

"A while back, my wife and I were going through some difficult times. It didn't last very long, but long enough to cause some damage. Unfortunately for me, I found solace in the wrong place. I got too close to a lady. One thing led to another… I fell for her. We ended up having an affair."

"Oh dear," Pastor Martin said, but he stopped in his tracks because he did not want to sound too judgemental.

"When things got back to normal with my wife, I ended the affair. She then claimed that she was pregnant by me. She tried to blackmail me. I convinced her to do a DNA test. Fortunately, the test confirmed that I was not the father, and I was able to put it all behind me."

"Did you tell your wife?"

"No, I didn't. I didn't want to hurt her."

"Why are you telling me this now, then?"

"Julie is threatening to tell the whole world if I don't get her back into the choir."

"She's blackmailing you? Are you kidding me?"

"No, I tried talking to her, but she refused to listen."

"Well, Pastor Kweku, we need to do the right thing. We cannot allow sister Julie into the choir. She has proven that she is not really converted. She needs to truly repent. I know it's not going to be easy for you. But we, as leaders, need to lead by example. We can't allow the likes of sister Julie to have control over us. You need to come clean. You need to tell your wife and confess before the church. That way, sister Julie and all the rest of them will never have a hold on you."

Pastor Kweku was sweating. He had no choice. He knew that his family was going to go through turbulent times.

"I have discussed it with Rita and we agree that this is a good time for me to resume my activities in the church. It's a pity it has to end like this. I think a lot of people in the church will agree that you did a great job in my absence. But I'm sure that once you've sorted out your difficulties, you will come back stronger. I want you to know that you have my and Rita's support. We will always be there for you."

"Thank you so much, Pastor Martin."

"Oh, one more thing. I'm going to take over the classes with Adam and Oliver for the time being. Just while you sort things out."

"They are due to come tonight."

"How are they getting on?"

"Well, I don't see much progress in them. They have not made any commitment whatsoever."

"Have you noticed any change of attitude or anything else that's positive?"

"No, not really. Except for last week, when they seemed to be a bit more focused for some reason. They were asking questions about Michelle and Caroline. They even asked to attend church and meet all the youngsters."

"That's interesting. We'll try to arrange that. Maybe instead of isolating them, they should join the youth group."

Pastor Kweku remained silent. He was thinking about the storm that was about to engulf his family and shivered.

***

After the confession, Pastor Kweku found himself in the pub, meeting with old friends. They had been part of his life before he became Christian.

"Long time, no see, Kweku."

"Show some respect; he is a pastor now."

"What's bringing you to your sinful heathen friends? You're not supposed to mix with us, your holiness."

"Come on, guys, it's not like that."

"How come you remembered us today?"

"I just wanted to connect with you guys, see how you are all doing."

"Suddenly, just like that?"

"We know you; you never do anything for nothing."

"Have they thrown you out of the pulpit? Is that why you're running to us?"

"Not at all."

"And how's the wifey and family?"

"They're fine."

Pastor Kweku could not go home straight away and face his wife; he was too distressed. He started drinking and could not stop. But eventually, he had to make his way home.

***

Back home, Fifi was in a state of febrility. It was getting late and her husband had not called to let her know what was holding him up. Even more worryingly, he had been acting very strange lately. The worst part was that he would not even talk about it. That is what worried her the most. They usually shared and spoke about everything. But this time, he would not say a word. He eventually arrived home and tried to tiptoe his way to his study. But Fifi was waiting for him.

"Where have you been?"

He had his back to her. He dared not look at her. She came closer to him.

"You reek of alcohol," she said in disbelief.

She had never seen him inebriated in all years they had been married. What on earth was going on?!?

"We need to talk. Open up."

"Not now; I'm too tired. I need some rest. We'll talk when I wake up."

"I'm not waiting a second more. You better talk. And fast."

He knew he could not run away from reality. He could not postpone the inevitable.

"I had an affair."

"What?"

Her world came crashing down. She thought they had it all together. There was trouble in paradise.

"How could you do this to me?"

"I'm so sorry. It was all a mistake."

"So, you mean to say that when you kissed her, it was a mistake? When you touched her and removed her clothes, it was still a mistake. When you found yourself in bed with her, it was a mistake yet again. It was all a mistake. Right?"

She was now sobbing.

"I'm sorry," is all he could say.

"Nothing could make you stop. Not even the thought of me. Or your family. Or better still, God."

"Please forgive me."

"You threw all of this away for what, a few minutes' pleasure? How selfish is that?!? You only thought about yourself. You forgot about me, your family, and all the rest of it."

Pastor Kweku did not know what else to say.

"So why are you telling me now?"

"Julie is threatening to go public with this if I don't help her get back into the choir."

"Oh, I see... So, it's not really your conscience that got you to confess. You were forced to do it."

Fifi ran out of the room. Just then, Pastor Kweku saw his daughter Michelle standing at the door, looking alarmed. She also ran out of the room. Why was his life so complicated?

***

Michelle went to her mum.

"Mum, are you alright?"

"I'm okay."

"No, you're not. I can see the tears on your face."

"It's nothing, sweetie."

"I heard you and Dad arguing."

"It's nothing to worry about, dear."

"Are you having problems with Dad?"

"It's nothing to worry about, Michelle. It's nothing we cannot sort out."

Michelle had never seen her parents argue in such a way. They were a close-knit family. The only arguments that happened were among the kids. She knew this had to be pretty serious.

Anyway, it was late, so she went to bed. She was tossing and turning and could not sleep. She had several friends whose parents had got divorced. She was afraid that the same might happen to her parents. 'Oh Lord, keep my parents from divorcing,' she prayed. Eventually, she fell into a deep sleep.

Chapter XXIV | Made in Chelsea

Very early in the morning, Keisha, Tanya, and Divine all moved to Chelsea to get away from the killer. They ordered a cab and their departure went unnoticed. Detectives Kelleher and Osborne (who had fallen asleep in the car) failed to see them leave the property.

The house that Divine rented was imposing. It was situated between South Kensington station and Gloucester Road station. Right in the heart of Chelsea, it was buzzing, affluent, and posh – the perfect hideaway for the mother and daughter. Tastefully decorated, and south-facing, it had a period charm.

"This is a magnificent property, Divine!"

"It's stunning." Tanya added, full of awe.

"Yes, that's why I went for it."

"I always wanted to know how it feels to live in Chelsea, you know, like the reality show *Made in Chelsea*."

"What's that?"

"It's a TV series that follows the lives of a group of twenty-something socialites. A bit superficial and out of touch with our everyday reality, if you ask me."

"But that's the point, Mum. I don't need to watch a programme that depicts my own life. What's the point of that? It's just a glimpse into the lives of the rich and beautiful," Tanya stated with a tinge of exasperation.

"Whatever, Tanya," Keisha said, and rolled her eyes.

Divine was delighted to have them as guests. It meant that she had some company when exploring London and other areas if time permitted. She had even thought about short trips to European cities, but the COVID-19 situation prevented her from doing so.

"By the way, I've arranged for us to meet up with Pastor Rita this afternoon for tea and scones," Keisha said to Tanya.

"Who is she?" asked Divine.

"She is our pastor's wife. We haven't seen her in a while because she's not been well."

"Mum, can Divine come with us?"

"I don't think that's a good idea. You know that Pastor Rita is unwell and also they don't know each other."

"I would love to come, but I'm meeting Sean later, so I won't be able to make it, anyway. But thanks, Tanya."

"Oh, that's a pity. You would love her."

"Tee wants you to go everywhere with her," Keisha said with a laugh.

"I know, right?" Divine laughed in response.

***

"Pastor Rita! I've missed you so much! I'm so happy to see you," Tanya said, beaming.

Tanya rushed to hug her, but Keisha reminded her about social distancing – particularly given Pastor Rita's condition. She looked so frail; the opposite of the strong woman she used to be. She attempted a weak smile. It took all of her strength to sit up straight. Tanya was alarmed. She could see the deterioration and how the disease was taking its toll on her.

"How are you feeling now?"

"Tee, let Pastor Rita catch her breath. Sorry, Pastor Rita, she is so excited to see you."

"I know, I understand. I've missed you both, too."

She stopped to breathe. In truth, she was happy to see them, but she wasn't sure whether it was a good idea. She was feeling so weak. Today was a particularly bad day.

"How is the treatment going?"

"It's gruesome, heavy going," she said with a little shortness of breath. "And this excruciating pain! Sometimes I'm left without words. But then, the grace of God upholds me and carries me through. I cry out to Him and then peace surrounds me. I feel the love of God so strongly."

"God will heal you, Pastor Rita," Tanya stated with so much conviction and youthful exuberance.

"Amen to that, Tanya."

"Amen, Tee," her mum acquiesced.

"You must be very excited about your competition win?" Pastor Rita asked with a smile. She wanted to deflect the attention to something other than herself.

"We were, and still are, ecstatic! It was such a beautiful thing. We are blessed to have Jay."

"You all did it, the entire choir."

Pastor Rita did not want all the credit to go to one man.

"Zack did exceptionally well with the songs he picked, the way he conducted the choir, and his leadership," Keisha said.

"That's true, he did it with such dexterity... You all made us so proud and represented the Lord and the ministry so well. The Lord will take you all higher. This choir will go far, watch this space," Pastor Rita said, mustering some strength.

"When are you coming back, Pastor Rita?"

She was taken by surprise by the question. Keisha understood her embarrassment and tried to help, as Tanya was very curious.

"Pastor Rita doesn't know for sure, but hopefully soon. Honey, go and get some water for us from the fridge."

"I also have some of the scones you like so much, Tanya."

Keisha obviously wanted some time alone with Pastor Rita, and she did not want her daughter around.

"Tell me the truth, Pastor Rita. What's the prognosis?"

"It's 50/50, they say. I could beat it or die quickly. I'm taking things one day at a time and living each day as it comes. With faith. Trusting God always. Fighting the good fight. Never giving up. Believing the report of God, not the report of man."

***

It was so touching. Keisha wished she could hold Pastor Rita and give her a big hug. She was grateful that she was even allowed to see her. Keisha was trying hard to hide her tears. As they left the pastor's place, she was wondering whether it was the last time they would see her. They both resolved to take some more time to pray for Pastor Rita. They had always relied on her, her strength and even her faith. But she was the one who needed their prayers this time around.

***

Zack went for his Muay Thai kickboxing session. He had not been for a while, even before the gospel competition. He was a bit rusty.

"Hey, guys, what's up?"

"We've not seen you for a while, man."

"Yeah. I've been busy, mate."

"Was it work-related?"

"No, my choir and I took part in a competition."

"Choir boy, eh?"

Zack could see Jason was slightly surprised. He probably could not reconcile doing Muay Thai kickboxing and singing in a choir.

"I just do kickboxing to try to keep fit, that's all. My passion is to lead a choir."

"Alright, I was just wondering."

Zack was thinking that he needed to share his faith more. All he talked about with these guys was kickboxing. It was about time he spoke about what mattered to him. And it was not the sport. "There was a time when my life was a mess. I had completely lost it. Didn't know where I was going. It was like I was being sucked into this big emptiness. Man, it was giving me nightmares. I had no peace. But the funny thing is that I grew up in a loving family and in church. My parents were ministers. But all of that couldn't keep me together, man."

"You seem to have grown out of it though, bro."

"I couldn't have done it on my own."

"What happened?"

"It took the Lord to take me out of the black hole I was in."

"Good for you," Jason said in a blasé way.

His body language said that he had heard these sermons before. And that to him, they were gimmicks to keep weak people weak.

"My grandmother used to tell me about the church and a 'Vicar of Dibley' wannabe or some crap like that, bro," Jason said and chuckled.

"I'm not talking to you about religion or a church. None of that could help. It's much bigger than that. It's about the God that sees within you. The God that knows you inside out. He knows your innermost thoughts. He's got your back. You're safe with Him. I asked Him to be part of my life. That's when everything changed. I found peace and a sense of purpose. It's not my work or kickboxing that gives me a kick. It's nothing but the Lord Jesus Christ. I instantly stopped having nightmares and feeling that I was falling into a bottomless pit. I found myself on safer grounds."

***

Jason was amazed. Suddenly, he was touched by Zack's words. To see a giant of a man like Zack talk about God, that was something. It got him thinking, maybe there was something there. Zack's words kept ringing in his ears 'He's got your back.' He knew more than anybody how much that meant, with all the violence going on in London. He had lost friends to stabbings and gang violence. He had joined the kickboxing club for self-defence. But he still could not shake off the fear he had when, coming back from his job as a bouncer in the early hours of the morning, he would walk down some of the dark alleys in the roughest areas in London. He was tormented by the thought that his life might be cut short by some violent act. He sure could do with God's protection. Maybe Grandma Margaret was right about this God stuff after all, who knows.

***

Zack had gone to meet up with Jay for a mentoring session.

"Hey, how are you doing, bro?" Zack asked Jay.

"I'm over the moon, man!"

"Why?"

"I've received invitations to sing at some events."

"Really? What events?"

"Well, one is a concert, I think."

"What type of concert?"

"I didn't ask, to be honest."

"That should've been your first question to them."

Jay immediately sensed that he had gone wrong somewhere.

"Let's talk about this for a moment."

Zack was his mentor and it was decisions like this where he could weigh in and help the young man.

"You have to decide whether you want to go secular or all-out gospel. You can't compromise on that. You also have to be aware that the ministry will not allow you to do both. Which do you choose?" Zack was getting straight to the point.

"I never even thought of that."

"That's my role as a mentor. To make you think. But ultimately, the decision is yours to take."

"I hear you."

"Have you already agreed to take on the gig?"

He was embarrassed, but he knew better than to lie.

"Ye-yes."

"I'm afraid you're going to have to go back on your decision if it turns out to be a secular event. Have you signed a contract, agreed to take part, or taken any money?"

"No, it hasn't come to that yet."

"You're good then."

Jay was relieved and grateful for Zack's advice. He needed it. He had made too many mistakes, and it had landed him in a lot of trouble. He was trying so hard to get out of this cycle of failure and non-achievement. He knew that his calling was to sing. He also knew that Abundant Life Ministries was giving him the chance of a lifetime to hone his craft and establish himself as a gospel singer. And, in time, he would make it into the gospel scene. That was the plan. He had been careless in his choices before and he needed to be mindful of that.

"I'll get back to them as soon as…"

"Keep me posted. If you need to talk, don't hesitate to get in touch, bro."

Just then, Zack received a text message notification. "An address in Chelsea? Time for a visit," he mumbled under his breath.

"I've got to go. See you in church," he said louder to Jay and turned to leave, not knowing that he was in for the shock of his life when his phone rang.

Jay realised how much he needed the guidance of an experienced mature Christian, like Zack.

***

Keisha and Tanya were at the house in Chelsea. They had returned from their visit to Pastor Rita. Keisha realised she wanted to speak to Zack after texting him, so was now talking to Zack on her mobile phone when the doorbell rang.

"Who is it?"

"The post! I've got some mail for you."

Keisha was distracted by her conversation with Zack. She did not question the fact that it was too late for the postman to do his rounds. Nor did she question the fact that none of them in the house was expecting any post. This was a temporary residence for all of them. Tanya was in her bedroom, reading. Suddenly, Keisha got the fright of her life when she opened the door.

"Don't move! Put your hands up!"

She saw a man pointing a gun at her. She immediately recognised him – Mark Forsythe. He looked slightly older and heavier than in the online photo. Keisha had not put the phone down, and Zack could hear everything. He was immediately alarmed, as he was fully aware that her life was in danger.

"Follow me without saying a word and don't try anything funny, or else you'll regret it."

Keisha was paralysed with fear. She was shaking. Tanya was upstairs, unaware of the drama unfolding in the lobby downstairs. The house was massive, so she could not hear the threats; she could not have heard anything anyway, as she had hearing problems. Her mother was being kidnapped while she was absorbed in reading one of her Bible stories.

"Get moving," he said in a threatening voice.

The shaking increased. She almost stumbled down the pathway. Was this the end for her?

"Get up! Don't play smart with me! If you're trying to slow us down, it won't work. No one is going to come and rescue you anyway…"

She did not utter a word. She needed to stay out of trouble. Knowing what she knew of him, this man meant business. She was worried about Tanya. She wondered how long it would take for Tanya to realise that she was gone.

In the car, he tied her mouth, hands, and feet with duct tape and threw a light blanket over her. Then he started driving. She had no idea where they were going. Her mobile phone had fallen somewhere, and she could not be sure where. She thought about her life. She was worried sick about Tanya. What would become of her, should she die? She had not been as organised as she should have liked. She regretted not having gone to the police earlier, as she had discussed with Zack. Distracted by their move to Chelsea, she had completely forgotten. This had proved to be a costly mistake. She had other regrets. She wished that she had told Tanya about Charlie and Pearl. Now her baby girl would not know about important issues from her past. She wished that she had overcome her fears and told Zack sooner that she loved him. Maybe she had unknowingly robbed herself of another opportunity to love and be loved. Also, it crossed her mind that she had left no will. Her affairs were not in order, that she knew. They drove for a while, though she was not sure for how long. Then she heard him speak to someone on speakerphone.

"I got her. She tried to outsmart us by moving to her friend's place, but I got her."

"Where are you?"

"About ten minutes away."

"I want you to take her to our facility in Stratford. You can take the back road."

"Do you have the postcode?"

"No, it doesn't have one, as it's part of the main facility. Go past the main building and then turn right – you'll see sort of back road. It's well hidden from the public's gaze. It's where the Special Unit Laboratory is located. There's no security there. Only a few of us are aware of its existence, so we will not be disturbed once we're in the grounds of the unit. I'm on my way. If I get there before you, you'll see my blue Vauxhall."

Was that Claire's voice? Keisha could follow their conversation and it was almost certainly hers. She could not believe her ears. How could she go to these lengths? She could never have imagined that her boss would be so cold and heartless. She was determined to get rid of her. She went into survival mode and began to pray. O Lord Jesus, save me from these murderers.

Chapter XXV | The Sea of Forgetfulness

Running out of the cab, Divine was in a hurry to find Keisha and Tanya home. She rang and rang the doorbell, but nothing happened. There was no answer. What was going on? She didn't have spare keys. She could see lights on but was met with silence.

She went in through an open door at the back of the house and locked it once she was inside.

"Keisha! Tanya!"

Still no answer. Total silence. She made her way upstairs. She went to Keisha's room, but it was empty. Then she went to Tanya's room and found her sleeping.

"Tanya!"

She had to call her several times before she woke up.

"Wake up, Tanya."

"Hey, Divine."

"Where's your mum?"

"She's downstairs."

"No, she's not. I didn't see her and I looked for her everywhere."

"I left her downstairs and came upstairs a while ago. I must have fallen asleep."

Divine knew immediately that something was terribly wrong. Keisha would never leave her daughter alone or leave without a word. She did not want to alarm the youngster. She did not want to call the police either, because she wouldn't know what to say. She tried phoning Keisha's number – it kept ringing, but she did not pick up the call. She had to get Zack's number. Who would have it?

"Tanya, do you have Zack's number?"

"Yes, I do. Is anything the matter?"

"No, not to worry."

"So, if you didn't see Mum downstairs, where could she be?" Tanya asked, curiously.

"I'm not quite sure."

"Here is his number."

She tried calling him, but the line was just ringing, unanswered. She was not sure what to do next.

"I have an idea! Church is on tonight, right?"

"Yes, it's prayer and Bible study."

"Let's go to church."

She was trying to get herself and Tanya out of the house. She feared that Keisha's life was in danger. She had ruled out the possibility that they would return for them, but they needed to move to a safer place as a precaution.

"Without Mum?"

"I'll leave her a note and tell her to meet us at the church."

"Oh okay, alright."

"Why don't you grab your stuff and I'll call us a cab."

***

Pastor Martin was in church, having returned from his sabbatical.

"Let's get started, folks. We have a lot to cover tonight. Come on, choir."

After the choir sang, it was time for prayer, followed by Bible study. It was a pleasant evening, but Divine could not really focus. She could hardly remember what the Bible study was about.

Then, suddenly, Pastor Martin stood before the congregation.

"Pastor Kweku would like to talk to us."

He got up and stood before the congregation, looking out at them for a few minutes. People started looking at each other, wondering what was going on.

"Brethren, you will recall that a few months ago, I preached a message about casting the first stone if we were without sin. I didn't realise that I would be concerned so soon. Sometimes, when preachers preach, we speak to ourselves first and foremost. I crave your indulgence and compassion. Alexander Pope once said 'To err is human, to forgive divine'. I have erred in many ways. There was a time during our marriage when things were not going so well. We grew apart and there were even talks of separation. I took a place of my own while my wife stayed with the kids for a few months. During this time, I had a brief affair with a woman. She did not have a love child by me, as some claim. It is no excuse that things were not working between my wife and me. We were still very much married. I made some poor choices. I have asked my wife to forgive me. She has forgiven me. Yes, it was difficult at first. But through the grace of God, she found the strength to forgive. I am grateful to God for that. The enemy thought he could use that against us. Today our marriage is stronger. I love my wife more than ever before. Proverbs 5:18 tells us to rejoice in the wife of your youth. I would not be the man I am today without her prayers and support. She believed in me and stood by me without fail. I want my wife, my best friend, and my African Queen, to share a few words with us."

Aunty Fifi walked majestically to the pulpit. She had a calm and peaceful air about her. She commanded respect.

"Good morning, church."

"Good morning, Aunty Fifi," the congregation responded.

"Praise the Lord! God has turned around what the enemy meant for evil. The enemy sent his agent, but he failed. We are more than conquerors in Christ Jesus! We are victorious! An agent of the enemy wanted to steal my husband away from me and wreck my home, but they did not succeed. I have chosen to forgive them. I have chosen to put them to shame. They will not destroy in minutes what took years to build. God indeed gave me the grace to forgive. For the Bible says in 1 Peter 4:8 'Above all, love each other deeply because love covers over a multitude of sins'. I love my dear husband. Yes, he fell, and what he did was wrong. But no one is perfect.

"Proverbs 24:16 also states 'though the righteous fall seven times, they rise again'. My husband has chosen to rise above this, to rise above the fall. I have decided to rise above his adultery. This will never destroy us. It has made us better and stronger. This has kept us humble. I can't lie to you; at one stage I was tempted to give up and file for divorce. But then who wins? There's a scripture that gave me strength in 1 Corinthians 10:13, 'No temptation has overtaken you except such as is common to man; but God is faithful, who will not allow you to be tempted beyond what you are able, but with the temptation will also make the way of escape, that you may be able to bear it'. I overcame the temptation to divorce because I was not going to let temptation overcome me! In Micah 7:19, it is written 'You will cast all our sins, into the depths of the sea'.

Some call it the Sea of Forgetfulness. Just like the Lord would, I have thrown it in the Sea of Forgetfulness. Amen!"

"Amen," the congregation responded.

People in the church erupted in cheers and applause. It was a beautiful scene. The pastors looked emotional. They had feared the worst. This drama had not caused a split after all. There was also relief in the congregation. Divorce was so rampant these days. They were happy that the Assistant Pastor and his family had not fallen victims. Michelle was the most relieved. She had prayed and prayed for her parents and God had answered her prayers. She was beaming. People gathered around the family as a show of support. Pastor Martin was proud of his congregation. They had grown. They had matured. They could show love and compassion. All the years of teaching and praying had paid off for them.

Later, Pastor Martin had a few things to take care of before retiring for the day. He had made an appointment with Adam and Oliver.

"Thank you both for accepting my invite today. I wanted to know how things are with you guys. Have you benefited from the weekly meetings you have attended over the last few months?"

They shook their heads, acquiescing.

"Is there anything you have to say?"

"We've learnt a lot. We've made some good friends here," Adam replied.

"Caroline, Michelle, Pastor Ben, and Tanya," Oliver added.

"That's good. I'm glad to hear it. Your meetings are coming to an end soon. Now, what did you have in mind?"

"We want to join the church. We're also thinking of joining the choir. I thought the competition was dope."

"Dope, eh?" Pastor Martin asked.

Pastor Martin was amused. But he was also satisfied with the way their lives were heading. Previously, they thought that the meetings had not had an impact on these youngsters. How wrong they were. They had come a long way – away from a life of crime. Pastor Ben had achieved his goal of reforming these youngsters. And not to forget the role Pastor Kweku played by teaching them to walk down the 'narrow road'. After the ordeal they had been going through with Rita's illness, this was good news. He could see their lives had turned around and he was delighted. Today had been a good day for him. He had a smile on his face. In fact, he felt that God was smiling at him.

"I'm happy to hear that you're settling nicely in our midst."

"That's right. Pastor Kweku has been organising for us to be picked up for church meetings and services."

"Well, it's not all about the church or the choir. What about the Lord Jesus Christ?"

"I have faith in the Lord," Oliver said quietly, not as outspoken as Adam. "I believe in Him."

"For me, well, I'm still thinking about it. You know…"

"Anyway, you need to feel ready yourself. It's not something you force, my friend. It's a personal thing."

"I got you, Pas'."

Adam and Oliver gave him the nickname, which they all found funny.

"If any one of you ever need to talk, you can come and see me," Pastor Martin added.

"Thanks, Pas'. We appreciate it."

The other issue he had to deal with was Julie. He had to expel her from the fellowship. She had refused to change and learn. It was time for her to bear the consequences of her reckless behaviour. He had already asked for her name to be removed from the church database. As hard as it was, he had to do it. She was far too lethal for his liking. But worst of all, she was unteachable; she just would not learn. It was the only unpleasant part of the ministry – having to deal with people who would not change and wanted it their own way. However, they could not continue to condone such evil behaviour. Something had to be done. 'It was God's way or the highway,' he would usually tell them.

Adam and Oliver left to meet Michelle, Caroline, and Pastor Ben. They had drawn closer together during this time, and sometimes Tanya joined them.

"You're so lucky that your parents didn't divorce, Michelle."

"I prayed so hard for that not to happen. I thank the Lord for coming through."

"For God is the rewarder of those who diligently seek Him," Pastor Ben said using a 'preacher' tone.

"Here we go again, Pastor Ben has spoken," Adam stated mockingly.

He liked to tease Ben.

***

Meanwhile, Divine and Tanya waited around for a little while after the meeting. Divine was really touched by the events of that evening, though it took her some time to really pay attention to what was going on. It had been a while since she had been in church.

"You have a lovely church. People are so loving and forgiving."

"Yes, we stick together. We're like family."

"That's so beautiful. You're very fortunate to have that. You should be grateful."

"Yes, I always thank God for our pastors and the church members."

"That's what you call a good support system."

"That's true; we always support one another. When someone cries, we all cry, and when someone laughs, we all laugh."

"That's the way it should be."

"There are some exceptions. But yes, in general, everyone is nice."

"Exceptions, like who?"

"Aunty Julie is something else."

"Ah, yes, Julie. I know what you mean. Was she not expelled from the choir?"

"She was asked to stay away for a whole year."

"Where is she?"

They looked around and could not see her. But then they spotted Jay and went to talk to him.

"Have you seen Zack, by any chance?" Divine asked.

"We spoke earlier on, but then he had to leave quickly after someone contacted him."

"Do you know who?"

"No, I don't. Why? Is there a problem?"

"No, we're just wondering whether Keisha is with Zack or not."

"I have no idea. Sorry I can't help."

Divine was in a dilemma. What should she do? Keisha had been reluctant to get the police involved. Maybe it was time for them to come in and intervene?

"We could contact Zack's parents."

"Do you have their number?"

"Yes, I do."

"Okay, I will go outside and call them."

"I'll go and see my friends in the meantime."

Tanya went to meet her group of friends. Divine decided to call the police and report her disappearance. However, she was told that it was too soon for them to do anything about it.

***

"Hey, guys."

"Hi, Tanya. We can see you're with Divine!"

"She's stunning and an amazing singer," commented Adam. He also thought that Tanya looked gorgeous. She had this mysterious beauty but also had this innocence.

"She's wonderful. We're both having a great time. What were you guys talking about?"

"About our parents – divorce and stuff."

"I'm so glad about your parents, Michelle," Tanya said, hugging her. "God is so good. It could have ended in a disastrous divorce, you know," she added.

"That's what I was saying to the guys before you joined us."

"I wish I knew where my father was," Tanya said, opening up to her friends.

"Have you ever met him?"

"No, but one day I will."

"My parents divorced a couple of years ago. My father left us to marry another woman. It was tough for us, for my mum," Oliver shared quietly.

"My dad has been in and out of jail. We rarely see him. My mum has had so many boyfriends I can't keep up with their names, mate," Adam joked.

"That must be so difficult," Caroline said, more understanding than usual, probably mellowed by the messages she had heard that evening.

"Well, you get used to it after a while. You sort of live your own life."

"Is that how you ended up hanging out on the streets and smoking marijuana? Do you see how God stepped in? He turned things around for you guys," Pastor Ben said.

"Preach, preacher," Adam teased him once again.

"But it's true," he insisted. "God arrested you both to keep you off the streets."

"You're right," Oliver agreed. "Some of our friends are in jail for one crime or another right now. We've decided to follow a different path for ourselves. We also promised Pastor Kweku that we would stop skipping school. We're going back to school in September."

"That's cool, guys," Caroline reacted with jubilation.

She had been taught the value of education by her parents. Her opinion of them had shifted. She was dubious at first, but now she could see that something had happened to the two teenagers. They had been the recipient of God's mercy. Pastor Ben's act of compassion had far more impact than any one of them could have imagined. "Pastor Ben, how do you feel about all this?"

"I'm truly awed by what God is doing. I'm so glad that I didn't seek revenge. It also proves that prison is not necessarily the best solution, you know."

"You have a point there. Our friends went to juve and came back hardened criminals. We've had to avoid them."

"Coming to this place is like a haven of peace, man. No violence, abuse, drugs, and the likes."

"You guys are fortunate. You've been blessed with caring and responsible parents and a safe environment to grow up and live in," Oliver commented.

They all felt for the two youngsters. They now understood where they were coming from, as they had opened up about their backgrounds.

"It's not too late for you guys. Don't forget about the Sea of Forgetfulness that Michelle's mum spoke about," Pastor Ben reminded them.

"Yep, we have a lot to throw in that Sea of Forgetfulness," Adam chuckled.

"Go on, throw it all in now," Pastor Ben encouraged.

"Now?" asked Adam.

"Yes, now," he repeated.

"And how do you do that?"

"Very simple," Michelle said. "For example, I throw the pain that my dad caused to my mum into the Sea of Forgetfulness. Your turn, Caroline."

"I throw into the Sea of Forgetfulness all the pain caused by my schoolteacher who is always putting me down. Now, you Pastor Ben."

"I throw into the Sea of Forgetfulness all the times that people laugh at me when I speak about God or quote the Bible. Your turn, Tanya."

"I throw all the abuse and bullying I got because of the way I look into the Sea of Forgetfulness." It reminded her of the mirror game. She felt compelled to continue.

"I'm free of their strange looks and reactions. I dare to dream. I dare to be different," she added daringly. She had adopted Zack's motto as her own. She felt even freer after that. Something had happened that she could not put into words.

"Over to you, Adam."

"I throw into the Sea of Forgetfulness the fact that my dad was never there for me. Over to you Oliver."

"I throw into the Sea of Forgetfulness my father leaving us and forgetting about us." Oliver almost had tears in his eyes.

Michelle, Caroline, and Tanya were clapping, delighted with this exercise, knowing that God had worked in a mighty way in all of their lives.

This turned out to be a powerful night, one that none of them would ever forget.

Chapter XXVI | The Kairos Moment

She could see that her mobile phone had fallen under the seat. Good, she thought. That was a piece of evidence that was left behind in case she did not escape alive. It would establish that she had been in the car at one stage or another. The automobile stopped abruptly. She almost fell from the car seat to the floor. Mark then dragged her out of the vehicle and removed the duct tape from her feet. Still holding her, he took her into the facility. Keisha did not even know that this unit existed. Something suspicious, or even criminal, was definitely going on.

He opened the unlocked lab door.

"Claire! Claire! Are you there?"

There was no answer. He called her on his mobile and she answered.

"Go down the corridor and turn left. I will meet you there."

As there were approaching the meeting place, Keisha opened her eyes in horror. She could see a group of people in an emaciated state. They looked sedated or drugged. They all looked to be of Asian origin. What was going on?!? Was this the human consignment that she read about in the document sent to her by mistake? Pieces of the puzzle were starting to fall into place. Claire suddenly emerged from upstairs. She was wearing a mask and gloves.

"Here, you're going to need these."

She handed him a mask and gloves. But offered none to Keisha.

"We finally caught up with you, Keisha," she said with wry amusement.

"I can see that you guys have been busy. What's going on here?" she asked her boss.

"What's going on is that you couldn't keep your mouth shut, could you? You've opened a can of worms. You had to poke your nose in where you shouldn't! Now, you have to face the consequences."

"I only did what was right for the safety of millions of people."

"And how do you think vaccines are made? Human experimentation happens a lot; it is well documented."

"Yeah, but those experiments were branded unethical."

"The advancement of medical science is only possible by taking such risks. That's how millions of people have been saved from deadly viruses and diseases. We have all benefitted from these experiments, no matter how unethical they were."

"You really make me sick."

"That's why you and I could never get along. You could never see the bigger picture. You're in your own little world."

"You're so cynical!"

"We would not have achieved anything if we didn't take those risks. It amazes me how naïve you are."

"I beg to differ. You're using your fellow human beings as guinea pigs. Have you thought of the impact on them?"

"We will all die of something one day. At least their death, if they die, will not be in vain. It will be for the benefit of all humankind."

"That's not our prerogative. God is the creator; it's for Him to decide when to end someone's life."

"Don't get religious on me. That's why you will never go far. You're a coward."

"I have a conscience, Claire. Something you never had much of."

"I have ambition and I know what it takes to reach the top. You're too busy hiding behind God! You will never know how to achieve success. That's why I'm at the highest level of management in our firm." While she was busy boasting, she could see Mark was getting nervous. He was probably not even aware of this trafficking business, and she assumed he wanted no part in it. He looked like he wanted to bolt as soon as he could, but probably already knew that he was already in deep trouble.

"So, what's going on in here?"

"Well, I might as well tell you, since you won't live to tell the story anyway," she replied coldly. "We're doing human experiments on those guys over there. We want to test the vaccine on them. We've had four rounds of testing so far. It's looking promising, but the problem is we've run out of time. We have to produce this vaccine sooner rather than later. We're already behind our competitors. As you can see, they have been given the deadly virus but have survived because we injected them with the vaccine. So, fingers crossed, it's fairly effective."

"Where on earth did you get all these people?"

"Mainly Asia. Nepal, Myanmar, Cambodia, Tajikistan, Kyrgyzstan."

"Basically, some of the poorest Asian countries. How did you bribe or blackmail them into doing this?"

"Well, they have been handsomely paid."

"Yeah, but they are risking their lives, so what's the point?"

"Let's say that their families will be well taken care of."

"What a consolation! So, the Helsinki Convention doesn't mean anything to you?"

"You're such a softie!"

"So, the Convention doesn't mean anything to you?" she insisted.

"Look, sometimes you have to compromise and accept the human cost for the advancement of medical science."

"It's unacceptable – that's why the Convention was implemented in the first place."

"You're living in Utopia, dearest. Come back to the real world."

"I can't believe you're so cynical. Life means nothing to you."

"That's where you're mistaken, it does. That's the reason why we do what we do. That's how millions of lives were saved through vaccines and medications. A small group of people had to be sacrificed for the greater good."

"To me, this is totally unethical."

"You think you know it all, but you're completely ignorant. Have you never heard of Edward Jenner and how he discovered the smallpox vaccine? He used an eight-year-old boy for his experiments. Neither the small boy nor his parents gave consent to this experimentation. Jenner is credited with saving millions of lives because, as you know, smallpox was a deadly virus at the time."

"That was another era and you know it."

"Yeah, but we have the same needs today. Deadly diseases and viruses are lurking around that require human experiments to enable us to develop their vaccines. Things have not changed."

"Well, there's no debating with you. If you don't see anything wrong with that, there's no point in continuing this conversation."

Keisha was fuming. Claire just shrugged her shoulders; it did not really matter to her what Keisha thought. The two women never saw eye-to-eye on anything, which is why they often collided.

"Mark, I want you to take Keisha and take a photo of her next to these guys."

"Hey, what are you doing?"

"We're going to pin everything on you. Say that you did the human experiments secretly for financial gain. The photo will act as proof. You also killed your childminder because she came across some documents that implicated you. That's why you never came forward to the police with any tangible information. You even disappeared from your home for a while to avoid detection. If you're wondering what documents I'm talking about, I've prepared some fake reports. I've also written a confession for you that you will type up and send to the police via your personal email. We will then pretend that your death was a suicide. Bingo, case closed!"

She sounded very satisfied with her plot.

"No one will believe that!"

"You won't be able to defend yourself because you will be dead, remember?"

"None of my friends will believe that story."

"It's not about what people believe. It's about evidence and proof. Once again, you're so naïve. All the evidence will point to you. Greed got the better of you. You fell for it and did the unthinkable."

Keisha was helpless. There had to be a solution somewhere. 'Oh Lord, please come to my rescue,' she prayed silently in her heart.

The three were startled by a noise.

Before they could react, Zack came charging in and hit Mark's hand. The gun fell on the floor. Zack managed to kick it in such a way that Mark could no longer reach it. The two men faced each other.

"I know you," Mark said.

Zack looked at him; he could not remember where he had seen this face before.

"Kickboxing in Crystal Palace. We did some sparring together a few months ago."

Keisha could see that Zack vaguely remembered as he hesitated. The emotions running over his face meant he was probably going over previous fights and trying to remember techniques he had used against him. Mark didn't look as fit or as athletic as Zack, but had the advantage of being heavier. After bobbing and weaving around each other, Zack moved in quickly and was able to neutralise his opponent, who was now breathing heavily, with a Muay Thai takedown from the clinch.

Keisha, in the meantime, was so shocked she remained rooted on the spot while Claire was waiting to see what happened with the fight.

Out of nowhere, Julie appeared on the scene.

"What are you doing here, Julie?" Keisha asked her in total shock.

"Surprised to see me, right? I've been following you guys since you moved to Chelsea. I also noticed that Zack had been following you. I had to make sure that he didn't see me. I was tailing him. He didn't even notice, which was just as well."

"Why were you following us?"

"You're the source of my problems and the enemy of my progress. You've been a real curse to me! I want to get back at you. I suppose you could say I'm seeking revenge."

"What have I done?"

"Since Zack arrived, he's only had eyes for you. Had you not been in the picture, I would have got his full attention."

"That's completely insane!"

She could not believe her ears. This was the person that had gone to the same church and sung in the same choir with her for years. They had attended numerous events together – weddings, baby dedications, baptisms, picnics, and choral performances. She knew that Julie was a difficult person, but she would never have branded her a criminal. Right now, she was a total stranger.

"That's what you think. Anyway, I'm here to help Claire with her plans, which I thought were brilliant."

"Have you lost your mind?"

"Not at all, love."

"But it doesn't make sense! Zack doesn't even love you and he never will."

"If I can't have him, you can't have him either."

Claire and Julie were now trying to grab Keisha and put her with the individuals taking part in the experiments. She did her best to fight them off and, with a lucky push, she managed to escape and run. She was faster than the two of them and after rounding a corner, found a door unlocked that she pulled open and entered the room. As she found a table to hide behind, she realised she was sweating profusely.

***

Zack had the opportunity to put into practice some of the Muay Thai strikes he had learnt. He was a much better kickboxer than Mark. His artillery of strikes was more diverse and complete than that of his rival. Yet, he chose not to fight. He had taken on Thai kickboxing for exercise, not to actually use it on someone. His sole purpose was to protect Keisha and save her life. All he had to do was to ensure that Mark was kept under control and remained harmless.

"Give it up, Mark. Just stop! You guys have been caught."

"You're wrong, mate. I'm gonna get rid of the both of you!"

"Not a chance! You'll have to get past me first."

"No worries," he said, really believing that he could overpower Zack.

"I see you're stubborn. But you're no match for me and you know it!"

Mark would not listen. He had a lot to lose. He did not want to go back to jail. No way! He was fighting for dear life. Zack had to use the body lock technique to stop him. However, Mark would not easily give up. Zack simply used the two-hand head control on his opponent. Unfortunately for Mark, he had an old injury that he sustained in prison, which caused an untold amount of pain.

"Aaaargh!!!"

Mark whimpered and contorted in pain, unable to fight anymore as he lay on the floor. They were out of danger.

Zack went looking for Keisha.

"Keisha! Keisha! Where are you?!?"

There was no response.

"Keisha! It's me!"

Keisha came out of her hideout. She ran to Zack and threw herself into his arms.

The police arrived at the scene, holding both Claire and Julie.

"How come the police are here?"

"I called them before I made my entrance."

"Can you confirm that these two women are involved?" a police officer asked.

"Yes, they are," Zack answered without hesitation.

The officer read them their rights.

"You do not have to say anything. But it may harm your defence if you do not mention when questioned something which you later rely on in court. Anything you do say may be given in evidence."

"You will have to come to the police station to make a statement," the same officer said to Keisha and Zack.

***

Keisha and Tanya were sitting at home in Finsbury Park. She had promised herself at the lab facility that if she came out alive, she would not keep anything from her daughter any longer, no matter how hard it was.

"We've got to talk, Tee."

"You sound serious. Have you finally agreed to marry Zack?"

"Tee! It's not about that at all!" She was taken aback.

"Okay."

"You know, I didn't tell you how Pearl died."

"How did she die?"

"She was murdered by some people who were trying to get rid of me."

"What? Are you for real?!?" Tanya said, alarmed.

"But don't worry, the assassins got caught and are heading straight to jail."

"Good for them!"

"We also need to talk about what happened years ago."

"Oh, what happened?" Tanya was curious.

"I've got to tell you this. You had a big brother called Charlie."

"Oh really? Where is he? With my father?"

Keisha stayed quiet for a while. She breathed deeply.

"Your father and I had a huge argument. He didn't believe that you were his daughter because of your beautiful blue eyes. And so, I rushed out of the house and did not realise that your brother had followed me. I reversed the car and hit him. He was killed instantly. It was a terrible accident."

"What? He died?!?"

She did not even notice the cause of the argument. She was in total shock.

"I'm so sorry, baby girl. Yes, he died. I know it's a lot to take in, Tee."

"Why… why am I just… just learning this now?" she asked, the grief almost choking her words, tears in her eyes.

"I didn't want to hurt you, my love."

"But I feel like you hid a big part of our lives from me. I always thought I was an only child."

"I'm sorry, I should have told you sooner. But I thought it would hit you too hard. I wanted to protect you from the pain."

Tanya then remembered the scene in the church earlier on and her strength was renewed.

"You know what? Let's throw it all in the Sea of Forgetfulness."

"What's that?"

She proceeded to explain what had happened in church with Aunty Fifi and her group of friends. "Good idea, Tee. Let's do that."

They both felt better. The past wouldn't haunt them any longer. Tanya took it all in her stride. She had come a long way from the shy and frightened girl she was a few months earlier. Since she played the mirror game with Divine, she was no longer worried about her looks. They had both learnt a great deal over the last year.

***

Keisha arranged to meet Zack. She had decided that life was too short to continue entertaining her fears. Her former boss might have been right about one thing, she was risk-averse by nature. But this was about to change. He had arrived with a red rose and a fruit basket.

"Will you marry me?" he asked, looking into her eyes.

This was the 'Kairos' moment, the moment of truth.

"Yes, I will!"

She did not waste time either. They were both ecstatic, elated.

"You know, from the time I saw you, I knew that you were the one," Zack said, smiling.

"Oh really? Do you know that Tanya had a dream a few months ago? She dreamt that someone was trying to kill me and that you came to the rescue. She was convinced that this was a message from God. I think she might have been right, you know."

"She was right. You should have paid attention. We could have been engaged months ago. You were too busy playing hard to get," he said jokingly.

"I wasn't ready. But, anyway, that's in the past. The most important thing is that we are engaged now."

Upstairs, Tanya was relieved. She said her prayers and thanked the Lord that she had been reunited with her mother. Soon enough, she was dreaming and could hear her mum whispering into her ear: "Sweet dreams, Tanya."

The End

COMING SOON!
DREAM BIG, TANYA

www.ingramcontent.com/pod-product-compliance
Lightning Source LLC
Chambersburg PA
CBHW071601080526
44588CB00010B/975